"We cannot finish the Great Commission without words" may be my favorite statement from *A Woman's Words*. This book does an incredible job of showing how inviting and investing in others takes not only our actions but also our speech. How else are we to evangelize, edify, encourage, and educate others in God's truth? As I read Chrystie's fantastic book, I found myself evaluating my own speech and considering how I use my words to point those around me to Christ. I pray that you have the same experience.

—KANDI GALLATY, author of *Disciple Her*

A WOMAN'S
WORDS

Getting to the Heart of Our Speech

CHRYSTIE COLE

A STUDY FROM
EZER

A Woman's Words: Getting to the Heart of Our Speech

ISBN: 9781794619418
Library of Congress Control Number: 2019932460

Design and illustrations by Madei Click

GRACE CHURCH
2801 Pelham Road
Greenville, SC 29615, USA
www.GraceChurchSC.org

CONTENTS

ACKNOWLEDGMENTS

This book is the fruit of many men and women who love Jesus and are committed to seeking and communicating his truth. First and foremost, thank you to the teaching team who undertook this project several years ago: Chris Curtis, Virginia Griffin, Jim Taylor, and Bill White. Your willingness to give of your time and energy to discuss the topic of words and its relevance in the lives of women provided the framework for much of this study.

Thank you to the Pastoral Advisory Team: Mike Chibbaro, Chris Curtis, David Delk, Jim Taylor, Bill White, and Matt Williams for your dedication to providing wisdom, insight, biblical clarity, and feedback on this study. Your commitment to loving, serving, and equipping the women of Grace Church is both humbling and profoundly encouraging.

To Ruthie Delk: I am incredibly thankful for your willingness to hole up in a cabin with me for an entire week to help me restructure, bring additional clarity, write reflection questions, and push the final revision of this study across the finish line. Your talent, the way you think, your ability to make content more accessible, and your passion for discipling women is a tremendous blessing to Grace Church.

Thank you to the women of Grace Church who dedicated their time to serving as test readers: Amy Kennedy, Barbara Dansby, Carolyn Berg, Charnise Mangle, Christy Peterson, Elisabeth Ingram, Gina Kincaid, Jessica Sterling, Jill Jennings, Cindy Barwick, Johndra McNeely, Kari Buddenberg, Katie Buckingham, Kayla Burns, Kelly Childress, Keri Geary, Kerry Sweeny, Kristi Stallo, Kristin Ellis, Laura Roe, Lauren

Tingle, Leslie Baxley, Lisa Troup, Lisa Yerrick, Lori Fay, Missy Lynch, Melanie Clint, Melinda Davidson, Mia Huffman, Monique Cook, Laurie Campbell, Nathalie Richard, Patti Massullo, Shannon Wilson, Sherry Gilliland, Stephanie Wood, Susan Jenkins, Tiffany Guerrero, Julie Cook, Tonia Hawkinson, Tracy Newkirk, Trina Thiry, Wendy Bosier, and Rachel Asire. Your feedback, encouragement, constructive criticism, and insights are always invaluable and shape much of the thoughts and direction of the study.

The backbone of this study is the prayer team who was faithfully committed to carrying this project to the Lord in prayer. Thank you to Adriana Avila, Amy Kennedy, Betsy Killins, Chappell Hughes, Glynis Lowrance, Hope Bray, Jane Wall, Joan Adams, Cindy Barwick, Julia Taylor, Kerry Sweeny, Kristin Ellis, Lacey Allston, Leslie Bennett, Nathalie Richard, Rose Marshall, Cindy Chibbaro, Shannon Wilson, Shari Horner, Stephanie Clarey, Virginia Vanvick, Virginia Griffin, and the countless others who were praying that I never knew about. The knowledge that you were praying, and your timely notes of encouragement, were a constant source of hope and strength throughout this endeavor.

Thank you to Abby Keith for contributing her time, energy, and writing skills to editing the study. Thank you to our communications team: Scott Mozingo, Tish Pitman, Madei Click, Matt New, Megan Burleson, and J.J. Puryear for your attention to detail, creative skills, and commitment to excellence.

Thank you to the women of Grace Church who lead our Ezer studies, who are committed to the work of intentional discipleship, who are willing to discuss sensitive and difficult subjects with one another, and who lead with courage, humility, and vulnerability. Thank you for faithfully carrying out the mission of the Ezer ministry. And finally, thank you to the women of Grace Church who participate in each Ezer study, who hunger for spiritual truth and desire to grow in spiritual maturity as followers of Jesus Christ.

01

WORDS MATTER

Then the Lord God said, "It is not good for the man to be alone. I will make a helper who is just right for him."

Genesis 2:18

A DIVINE CALLING

Words are powerful. From the time we are first able to understand them, they help create, shape, define, and explain our reality. They help us engage and understand the world around us. Words are essential to the relationships we build, the work we do, and the problems we try to solve. They have the power to create as well as destroy. They have the power to strengthen and encourage or the power to demean and demoralize. The impact of words transcends culture, socioeconomic status, educational background, and gender. Men and women alike use their words in ways that are both constructive and destructive. So why a study on women and their words? We look to the book of Genesis for answers.

In Genesis 1:26, the Lord determined to make man in his own image. So he created human beings to be a reflection of himself and to represent him to the rest of creation (Genesis 1:26–28). Humanity was created for a specific and divine purpose—to represent God and to be a blessing to the world. Genesis 2 continues this theme, giving specific insight into God's rationale for creating the woman:

> Then the Lord God said, "It is not good for the man to be alone. I will make a helper who is just right for him."
>
> Genesis 2:18

The Lord looked at his labor and declared it to be good. But then he looked on Adam, who labored alone in the garden, and for the first time declared, "It is not good." So God determined to make a helper, an *ezer-kenegdo*, for Adam.

The Hebrew word *ezer* means one who helps, one who brings that which is lacking to the aid of another. An *ezer* assists another toward accomplishing a goal. Thus the word *ezer* actually connotes an inherent strength. The word *kenegdo* means corresponding to. Joined together, *ezer-kenegdo* means an essential counterpart or corresponding strength.

An *ezer* is someone who is for you, an ally—someone who supports, aids, rallies to your cause, and brings you strength. And God entrusted his *ezer* nature to women that they might reflect his character in this distinct and powerful way. [1]

The word *ezer* is used twenty-one times in Scripture: twice in reference to the creation of woman and three times as a military term. But it is used sixteen times in reference to God as our *Ezer*, as the one who brings strength and life to his people through relationship with him.

The life-giving strength of God's *ezer* nature is on display in Psalm 146:

> Don't put your confidence in powerful people;
>   there is no help for you there.
> When they breathe their last, they return to the earth,
>   and all their plans die with them.
> But joyful are those who have the God of Israel as their *helper*,

whose hope is in the Lord their God.
He made heaven and earth,
the sea, and everything in them.
He keeps every promise forever.
He *gives justice to the oppressed*
and *food to the hungry.*
The Lord *frees the prisoners.*
The Lord *opens the eyes of the blind.*
The Lord *lifts up those who are weighed down.*
The Lord loves the godly.
The Lord *protects the foreigners among us.*
He *cares for the orphans and widows,*
but he *frustrates the plans of the wicked.*
The Lord will reign forever.
He will be your God, O Jerusalem, throughout the generations.
Praise the Lord!

Psalm 146:3–10 (*emphasis author's own*)

This psalm depicts the *ezer* nature of God as one who comes to the aid of those in need—the poor, the hungry, the oppressed, the outcast, the downtrodden, the foreigner—those who are in a position of vulnerability, weakness, and dependency. He brings strength, aid, refuge, nourishment, and support. God is accessible, knowable, and available to those who have nothing to offer him in return. He enters into their lives and brings all of his resources to bear in such a way that they become more of who he intends them to be. Those who have God as their help, as their *ezer,* are blessed (Psalm 146:5).

This divine calling has been entrusted to women. God created women to reflect his *ezer* nature—bringing strength, life, aid, support and refuge in and through their relationships. This is the God-given power of femininity, which he intends us to use for the good and blessing of others. Using our strength to come to the aid of another, as their ally, cannot occur apart from relationship with them. Words have a huge impact on forming and developing relationships. This means living out God's call as an *ezer* will happen, in large part, through the words we use—whether written or spoken.

While being an *ezer* is the same calling for all women, there is freedom of expression according to each woman's individuality and season of life. A woman's individuality—her personal uniqueness—includes personality, background, upbringing, experiences in life, sin struggles, strengths, and weaknesses. Each of these shapes how a woman lives out her *ezer* calling. But a woman's season of life—whether she is a student, a wife, a mom, a single, a working woman, a caregiver for a disabled family member or aging parents, a divorcée, a widow, an empty-nester, a grandparent—also informs how and with whom she lives out her calling.

The *ezer* calling is reflected through each woman's capacity to invite, nurture, and partner with those in her life. These capacities are simply attributes of God that reflect his character. Inviting is the gateway that brings us into relationship with others. This is where the *ezer* calling begins. *Inviting is welcoming others into a safe, life-giving, and unselfish relationship where they can find strength and refuge.* As a woman invites those around her into this type of relationship, she is reflecting the hospitable nature of God.

Nurturing is caring for and fostering the development of another with the goal of independence. A woman who nurtures others is bringing all of her resources, including her words, alongside another in such a way that enables them to flourish. A woman's capacity for nurturing is not dependent upon whether or not she is a mother. This attribute of God can be reflected in all of her relationships.

While nurturing is bringing your resources alongside another to help them become more of who God desires them to be, *partnering is aiding another in accomplishing a goal.* In partnering, a woman brings all of her skills and resources alongside another, carrying real weight and responsibility in such a way that the other person feels a portion of the burden lifted and a sense of true partnership in accomplishing the goal together.

These perfect capacities of God are specifically reflected in women, but as a result of the fall in Genesis 3, the reflection of God's *ezer* nature through femininity is distorted. Rather than coming alongside others and bringing strength to them, we corrupt this calling by leveraging our strength and influence over others instead. Rather than living in an interdependent relationship with others where we bring strength and life, we withdraw from relationships in self-protection or we overpower our relationships through self-promotion. Both self-protection and self-promotion are the outworkings of the core sin of autonomy—our desire to be self-governing and have moral independence in our lives— which impedes our ability to live out our *ezer* calling. [2]

Words are not just a woman's issue—every man, woman, and child struggles to control the tongue. But because of the distinctiveness of a woman's calling, to bring strength in the context of relationship, it is imperative to consider our words and how we, as women, struggle to speak in ways that reflect our calling. We demonstrate our autonomy by using our words to control our circumstances and steer our lives, or the lives of others, in the most favorable direction. More often than not, this manifests itself in the life of a woman through some manner of self-promoting or self-protective speech.

I remember my own efforts at self-protection a few years ago when my husband was making a decision I had convinced myself would be harmful for our family. I badgered him, asking question after question. I belabored points—rehashing them over and over again. The more fearful I became, the more withdrawn and curt my words became. The decision he was making would cause the two of us significant discomfort, but ultimately it would be the best possible decision for our son. The problem wasn't his decision; it was that I didn't like his decision—I didn't want to make the sacrifices his decision would require. My allegiance in that season was to myself and my own desires, and my words were the evidence of my devotion.

Self-protective speech can take many forms: deflecting, blame-shifting, evading, telling half-truths, rationalizing or justifying our actions. Below are a few examples of self-protective speech:

- It's the woman who has never experienced the affirming love of a father, and who is deeply critical of her own husband. Deep down she fears she is unworthy of love, so rather than risk being vulnerable to him, she finds it easier to tear down and criticize.

- It's the woman who blame-shifts or deflects during conflict. She would rather the other person feel guilty and be wrong than have to bear the responsibility of her own failings.

- It's the woman who won't take action without asking a thousand questions—clarifying and re-clarifying—not out of a desire to understand but because she can't risk failure.

- It's the single woman who verbally trashes men in order to feel better about being single.

Self-promoting speech also takes many forms. It might look like bragging, which is simply an attempt to control others' opinions of us. This can happen in obvious or subtle ways; sometimes we even cloak our bragging behind a façade of spirituality or false humility, strategically inserting statements about our volunteer work into conversations with others. Maybe it looks like flattery—using insincere or excessive praise in order to endear others to ourselves. Perhaps we exaggerate details or even lie to others in order to elevate ourselves. Here are just a few examples of self-promoting speech:

- It's the young woman who is wounded by a breakup and attempts to win others to her side. She would rather elicit pity and vindication for herself, and incite anger and division among her peers, than be seen as unworthy or undesirable.

- It's the disenchanted wife who seeks out those who will jump on the husband-bashing bandwagon with her—validating her, affirming her frustration, legitimizing her complaints—rather than seeking those who will speak hard truth, challenge her perspective, and encourage a spirit of humility and oneness.

- It's the woman who discredits her coworker by subtly pointing out their weaknesses or failings, which just happen to point to her own strengths. She skillfully undermines her co-worker in an attempt to elevate herself.

- It's the mother who criticizes and blames the teacher for her child's failure in the classroom. She would rather destroy the teacher's credibility and reputation than have her child's struggles reflect negatively on her in some way.

- It's the woman who shares her opinion without first weighing her words. She doesn't take time to think about how what she says or the way she says it could impact the person. What she has to say is far more important than the person she is saying it to.

At the root of self-promotion and self-protection are our own self-centered desires, and *words are the tools we often use to satisfy those desires on our terms*. We exert our autonomy, using our words to manipulate others and control the world around us.

I am sad to say this reminds me of a conversation I once had with my husband. I remember I was irritated with him at the time; some of my frustrations were legitimate and some weren't. During this season, I wanted to buy something, but we were on a tight budget and I knew he would probably say no. One day I approached him and masterfully laid out my argument. I calmly and respectfully expressed my frustrations with him—weaving in elements of truth with elements of guilt and manipulation. I cloaked it in false humility, saying "I am sure it's probably just me," and then I made my closing argument by pointing out what I thought could help me—which just so happened to be what I wanted to buy. In the end, I got what I wanted—which, I am ashamed to admit, was to make my husband feel bad about what I considered his failings and to be able to purchase what I wanted. Shortly afterward, I got a nagging feeling in the pit of my stomach. I knew something wasn't right. After a few days and some self-examination, the Lord exposed the selfish motives of my heart, and I was able to go and confess them to my husband and ask for his forgiveness.

The insidious nature of this scenario is that I wasn't even aware of what I was doing at the time. It all made perfect sense in my own mind, and I felt completely justified in my thoughts, words, and actions. I was blinded, self-deceived. My allegiances were to myself and myself alone. I wanted what I wanted—vindication for my husband's alleged wrongs and to satisfy my desires for material gain. I sacrificed my husband on the altar of my own agenda. My allegiance in that moment fueled my words—conniving, scheming, manipulative—which ultimately reflected the character of Satan more than it did the Lord in whose image I am created.

The undergirding fact is we love ourselves more than we love God and neighbor. We want to create our own personal utopia—a world we are able to manage and control to ensure our ultimate happiness, comfort, and security. And we will sacrifice others in order to attain it. Ultimately, what all of this means is this: *Our words reflect our allegiance.* We are either devoted to ourselves and fulfilling our own agenda, which is autonomy, or we are devoted to God, submitting ourselves to his call on our lives and entrusting ourselves to his care.

The goal of this study is to explore the impact our words have on our calling as women. As an *ezer*, our calling is fulfilled through our relationships with others. Relationships are primarily built on words. And words will either strengthen and bring life to a relationship or they will destroy it. Words matter.

OUR WORDS

REFLECT OUR

ALLEGIANCE.

Questions for Reflection

1. Is there anything that surprises you about the definition of *ezer* and what it means to be a woman?

2. Self-promotion and self-protection are two ways our calling gets corrupted. Which of these is more characteristic of you?

3. If someone recorded all of the words you spoke in the last month—who would they say you are devoted to?

4. What is your own personal struggle with your words or speech?

02

WORDS SHAPE US

Words shape us. They shape what we believe about ourselves, what we believe about God, and what we believe about others. They frame our experience of reality and shape how we interact with others and the world around us. Abraham Heschel, a Jewish Rabbi who survived the Nazi Holocaust, understood this all too well. Heschel's daughter, Susannah, reflected on lessons her father taught her about the power of words, saying:

> "Words, he often wrote, are themselves sacred, God's tool for creating the universe, and our tools for bringing holiness—or evil—into the world. He used to remind us that the Holocaust did not begin with the building of crematoria, and Hitler did not come to power with tanks and guns; it all began with uttering evil words, with defamation, with language and propaganda. Words create worlds, he used to tell me when I was a child. They must be used very carefully." [1]

Words create worlds. In the case of the Holocaust, they shaped how an entire country viewed those of Jewish descent. Adolf Hitler spoke and his hate-filled words gave rise to evil and the eradication of millions of men, women, and children. Hitler's words tickled the ears and egos of his people. His words became the beliefs and practices of a nation. They created a world in which Jews could be dehumanized, robbed of their personhood and their dignity, and, ultimately, their very lives.

While it's unlikely any of us have been impacted by words to this degree, almost all of us have been wounded by the words of others. The words of others often play a role in shaping our beliefs about ourselves and ultimately the ways in which we interact relationally. In that sense, words create the worlds in which we live.

The first real memory I have of words seeming to shape my reality were spoken by my own grandmother. The memory is so clear I can still remember where we were when she said them. I was a preteen, maybe twelve or thirteen years old. We were walking down the beach when she put her arm around me and exclaimed in her Cockney British accent, "Man, ya gettin' fat!" Maybe she was being playful. Perhaps they were meant to be endearing. I know she didn't intend to harm me; she just didn't take time to consider the weight of her words and the long-term impact they could have on me.

Words are sticky. They tend to linger long after they are spoken. And wounds inflicted by words have a tendency to fester and persist for an entire lifetime. The world is full of walking wounded. Young and old. Male and female. Every race, nationality, and socioeconomic status. Even organizations rise and fall by them. Words do not discriminate. No one is immune to their power. No one escapes them. The evidence is all around us:

- Women who haven't been able to shake the harsh, condemning, or disapproving words of their own mothers—women whose lives are now marked by a wearisome quest for approval, accolades, and achievement.

- Men who lack confidence and are paralyzed in their adulthood not only by their mother's demeaning words, but also by her nagging and constant questioning, which they often perceive as her lack of confidence.

- Young women in an endless pursuit to find love and affection from a man due to the absence of directional, affirming, and stabilizing words from their fathers.

- Women who are discouraged and disillusioned by the words of those they considered friends and who now find it hard to trust others in their lives.

- Strong, capable women who have resigned from positions of leadership because of the nagging, criticism, henpecking, and gossip that wore them down over time.

- Husbands who have lost confidence and motivation after years of their wives pointing out flaws and weaknesses in thoughtless, disrespectful, and unhelpful ways.

- Students who have been isolated and ostracized by their peers on social media.

- Countless mothers who've been shunned for not homeschooling or breastfeeding or working or meeting current mainstream expectations.

- Churches that have split because of slander, gossip, criticism, and posturing.

- And far too many non-Christians who have rejected the Christian faith because they've witnessed or been subjected to the harsh and unkind words of professed believers—whether online or in person.

There is no doubt we have all been deeply wounded by the words of others, and the ramifications of those words stretch far and wide into our lives. Perhaps the most egregious impact of words is shame. The careless and/or harmful words others spoke over you when you were young often result in shame. Shame informs your self-perception. *You begin to believe what others have said about you is the truest thing about yourself, and then orient your life around that belief.*

Take a few moments to look at the graphic below:

This is the power words have in shaping us. While it is true these words have in some way shaped our stories, somewhere along the line, we adopted anothers' words as our own. The wounds once inflicted on us by another become self-inflicted wounds as we speak these words over ourselves time and again. *We are indeed engaged in a war of words—but the war is now within ourselves.*

The words my grandmother once spoke over me became a persistent thought that I was unworthy of love and acceptance. And for the last thirty years, these are the words I've spoken over myself time and time again. I began to think about myself as not good enough, thin enough, pretty enough, desirable enough, or worthy of love and acceptance—which led me to do all kinds of things to prove myself worthy, valuable, and desirable. The actions I took then shaped the trajectory of my life. They created the world in which I've lived my entire adult life.

Let that sink in for a moment. The words my grandmother spoke to me when I was twelve years old became my internal world, which was filled with the negative words I spoke over myself, which then led to the way I lived in the world on a daily basis.

We typically categorize self-harm as actions like cutting, binging and purging, drinking too much, engaging in pornogrpahy, and seeking affirmation and approval through promiscuous sex. But before any of these behaviors manifest themselves in a woman's life, they begin with words. The words others speak over a woman can become the

SHAME INFORMS YOUR

SELF-PERCEPTION. YOU BEGIN

TO BELIEVE WHAT OTHERS HAVE

SAID ABOUT YOU IS THE TRUEST

THING ABOUT YOURSELF,

AND THEN ORIENT YOUR LIFE

AROUND THAT BELIEF.

dominant way in which she views herself, which in turn shapes how she lives—all of which reinforces the shame narrative in her life. This is where we would do well to heed an oft-quoted proverb:

> "Watch your thoughts; they become words. Watch your words; they become actions. Watch your actions; they become habits. Watch your habits; they become character. Watch your character; it becomes your destiny." [2]

Take a few moments to think back over your own life. What words have others used toward you? How have those words shaped what you believe about yourself? What words seem to echo in your mind over and over? Maybe the word you hear is "fat" or "stupid" or "ugly" or "worthless" or "incompetent". Whatever words come to mind, it is likely you will find a direct correlation to the values that drive you in life— your core motivations, needs, fears—because the words that shaped your internal world also shape your external experience of the world.

Now think about the trajectory of your life. What have been some of the dominant themes? Maybe your life is defined by constant dieting and exercise. Or maybe you have an insatiable desire for knowledge and status. Or perhaps you can't leave the house without making sure you look your best. Or perhaps you are on the constant treadmill of trying to prove your value to others—whether as an employee, as a wife and mom, or as a child of God.

What actions are creating chaos or turmoil in your life? Beneath these harmful behaviors lies an inner belief you reinforce over and over again. This is where it is important to listen to yourself. What is your inner narrative? What is the story you are telling yourself about who you are? What words do you speak over yourself? Remember, words shape worlds. What you say eventually shapes how you live and what you believe.

Questions for Reflection

1. Abraham Heschel said that words create worlds. Have you ever thought about the power words have to create worlds? Give an example of a way you see this happening in the world around you.

2. What words did others say to you and/or about you when you were young? Write them across the face of the young girl below.

3. How have these words shaped what you believe about yourself?

4. What ongoing role could these words be playing in your life today?

THE SOIL THAT SHAPED YOU

Fridays are my day off. Early in my marriage, my husband would come home from work on a Friday and ask me what I did all day. This question often led to conflict between us because I was wounded and offended by the question. It was an innocent question on his part, his attempt to move toward me and connect with me. But what I heard was completely different from what he said. I heard him say that I was lazy, that I hadn't done anything of value, and that I needed to prove myself worthy of his respect and love through my accomplishments. This always led me to rattle off a long list of things I had accomplished throughout the day in order to validate myself in his eyes.

Why did I hear something different than what he actually said? Words spoken over me as a young girl gave birth to the belief that I was not good enough. This shame then gave rise to proving my worthiness through overfunctioning especially at work, in my marriage, and in my relationship with God. Those words also became filters through which I heard and perceived the words of others.

We are constantly evaluating the world around us and how we relate to it. Everything we hear and see is interpreted through our own filters. When another speaks to us, what they say travels through the filters of our past experiences, present reality, wounds and fears, knowledge and season of life, personal sin struggles and spiritual maturity, and level of respect we have for the person speaking. All of these factors combined becomes the soil in which our lives take root; it's the soil that shapes us.

The graphic below illustrates how what has shaped us impacts what we hear.

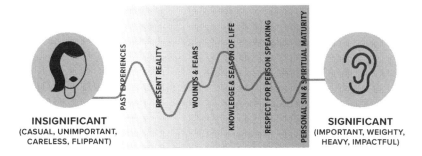

INSIGNIFICANT
(CASUAL, UNIMPORTANT,
CARELESS, FLIPPANT)

SIGNIFICANT
(IMPORTANT, WEIGHTY,
HEAVY, IMPACTFUL)

PAST EXPERIENCES — PRESENT REALITY — WOUNDS & FEARS — KNOWLEDGE & SEASON OF LIFE — RESPECT FOR PERSON SPEAKING — PERSONAL SIN & SPIRITUAL MATURITY

This graphic can help us in two ways. First, it helps us as *hearers* to understand why we are so easily offended by anothers' words. This is why my husband could speak something he deemed seemingly insignificant, but it ended up being hurtful and offensive to me. His words traveled through my upbringing, family of origin wounds, and fears of not being good enough, as well as the fact that as my husband, what he says carries significant weight.

How are your own filters interpreting or misinterpreting what another person has said? Rather than being reactionary, stewing, getting angry or retaliating, we must practice being gracious and believing the best of others. When there is a gap or misunderstanding in communication with another, we can choose to fill the gap with trust rather than suspicion—believing the best and asking for clarification when necessary. We can risk being vulnerable by telling them, "This is what I just heard you say. Is that what you meant for me to hear?"

Second, this graphic can help us as *speakers* because what we say is never received exactly as we intended. This is quite possibly one reason many conflicts occur. Perhaps this is why James encouraged us to be "quick to listen, slow to speak, and slow to get angry" (James 1:19b). Being slow to speak means you take time to think before you speak. You pause long enough to consider who you are speaking to and how they might receive what you are about to say. The words you speak are interpreted through their own filters—their past experiences, present reality, wounds and fears, spiritual maturity, and the respect they have for you. All of these contribute to how a person receives what you have said. While you are not responsible for what others hear, you are responsible for considering who you are speaking to, what you are saying, and how you are saying it.

Words are not insignificant. The words others have spoken to and about us have shaped how we view ourselves and how we live in the world. Likewise, the words we speak have the power to shape the internal and external world of others in our lives. We must carefully consider what we say. Words create worlds.

Questions for Reflection

Take a moment to think about the filters in the ear diagram and answer the following questions:

1. What past experiences might cause you to misinterpret things others say to you?

2. How can your present reality (circumstances) impact how you hear and respond to something someone says to you?

3. Think about a time you overreacted to something someone said to you. Why do you think you responded the way you did? What wound or fear contributed to how you heard what they said?

4. Think about a time someone overreacted to something you said. What filters might your words have traveled through, shaping what they heard? What could you have done or said differently in light of this?

5. How has your world been shaped by the words others have spoken to or about you?

6. How have you wounded others with your words? What type of worlds have you created for those in your sphere of influence?

03

THE ORIGIN OF WORDS

The lips of the godly speak helpful words, but the mouth of
the wicked speaks perverse words.

Proverbs 10:32

THE ORIGIN OF WORDS

I wish I'd had a hidden camera to capture the expressions on every
woman's face when I explained I was working on a study about a woman's words. It's pretty comical when I think back on it. Some women
sheepishly giggled. Others looked like deer in headlights. Some grimaced, nervously muttering something indistinguishable under their
breath. But almost every woman had a visceral reaction to the topic.
We instinctively know the power of our words. Why does this topic
produce such a nagging sense of unease and discomfort among us? In
order to understand why this is true, we must go back to the beginning
and see what Scripture says about the origin of words.

GOD SPEAKS

The Bible reveals a God who speaks. Before any human being was born or ever uttered a word, God existed.

In the beginning God created the heavens and the earth. The earth was formless and empty, and darkness covered the deep waters. And the Spirit of God was hovering over the surface of the waters. *Then God said, "Let there be light," and there was light...Then God said, "Let there be a space between* the waters, to separate the waters of the heavens from the waters of the earth." *And that is what happened.*

Genesis 1:1–3, 6–7 *(emphasis author's own)*

One of the first things we learn about God is that *he speaks.* God not only speaks, he was the first to ever speak. God created words; they flow from him. We also see a pattern emerge. When God speaks, creation responds (Gen 6–7, 9, 11, 14–15, and 24). His words are embedded with power. He commands the borders of the seas (Job 38:8–11), and by his command the morning appears and dawn rises in the east (Job 38:12). He shouts to the clouds and makes it rain, and he directs the lightning bolts to strike (Job 38:34). It is interesting and significant that the biblical authors present the idea that God uses words in his providential activity. When God speaks, things happen; what he says, comes to pass.

God's word produces fruit and brings many benefits. The psalmists declare God's word revives the soul, makes wise the simple, brings joy to the hearer, and gives insight to the living (Psalm 19:7–8). Psalm 119, the longest of all the Psalms, has one hundred and seventy-six verses entirely devoted to God's word, a magnificent picture of its life-giving power to produce joy (verse 2), delight (14, 16), hope (43), comfort in affliction (50), and peace (165). It upholds and sustains (116), protects from stumbling (165), provides good counsel (24), brings understanding (130), encouragement and strength (28), and a life free from shame

(6) and from sin (11). The psalmist ultimately finds life and renewal in God's word (25, 93).

But perhaps more striking than God's words preserved through Scripture is the fact that one of the clearest ways God speaks to us is through Jesus. Scripture tells us Jesus was the Word made flesh (John 1:14; Hebrews 1:2). John refers to him as the Word of life (John 1:1-4; 1 John 1:1); and the book of Revelation states his name is the Word of God (Revelation 19:13). Jesus is the personification of God's speech, expressing the very character of God—and he is full of grace and truth and life (John 1:14; 6:63).

SATAN SPEAKS

Scripture also shows that God is not the only one who speaks. Satan also speaks, and in Genesis 3, he chose a serpent as his mouthpiece. Genesis describes the serpent as the shrewdest of all the animals God made—intelligent, perceptive, subtle, cunning, and crafty. In essence, he was good with words and able to use them to cast doubt, skew the truth, and plant seeds of confusion.

> "The serpent was the shrewdest of all the wild animals the Lord God had made. One day he asked the woman, "Did God really say you must not eat the fruit from any of the trees in the garden?"
>
> "Of course we may eat fruit from the trees in the garden," the woman replied. "It's only the fruit from the tree in the middle of the garden that we are not allowed to eat. God said, 'You must not eat it or even touch it; if you do, you will die.'"
>
> "You won't die!" the serpent replied to the woman. "God knows that your eyes will be opened as soon as you eat it, and you will be like God, knowing both good and evil."
>
> Genesis 3:1-5

The serpent exercised great precision—bringing God's trustworthiness into question and putting a compelling spin on the truth. *He planted a seed of doubt, causing Eve to view God with suspicion.* He appealed to her desire to be like God and to gain knowledge of good and evil. But being created in God's image, Eve was already like God. And she already had knowledge of good. In fact, all she knew was good. She only lacked the knowledge of the evils of adversity and suffering and death. But with the hook baited, the enemy cast his line, and Eve sank her teeth into the forbidden fruit, which resulted in death and destruction. Isn't it ironic, that in the creation story, words are at the center of both life and death?

Scripture paints a grim picture of Satan. John declared Satan is a liar; there is no truth in him (John 8:44). Lying is his nature, his native tongue. The books of Job (1:6), Zechariah (3:1), and Revelation (12:10), depict Satan as the adversary who accuses and prosecutes humanity before God day and night. The apostle Paul calls him a cunning deceiver—one who is skilled and crafty with words—and who uses them to gain advantage over God's people, to seduce them and lead them astray (2 Corinthians 11:3).

Where God's words established order, Satan's words disrupted. Where God's words provided direction and established fellowship between God and man, Satan's words produced division, distrust, and rebellion. Where God's words were upright and true and would lead to life, Satan's words were deceptive and misleading and ushered in death. There is no doubt that when the enemy speaks, death, destruction, and chaos result.

WE SPEAK

God created men and women in his image, to reflect him and bring him glory (1:27). Genesis makes it clear that nothing else in all creation bears and reflects God's image like humanity, and one of the ways we reflect him is our ability to speak. The first human words recorded are Adam's, expressing his delight over God's creation of Eve as his counterpart and companion (Genesis 2:23). But then we have no more record of humanity's words until the short interaction between Eve and the serpent in Genesis 3. Through this brief dialogue, death and destruction, adversity and suffering, became an ever-present part of our human experience. One quick conversation and life would never be the same again. In that moment, everything changed— including how we use our words.

When the cool evening breezes were blowing, the man and his wife heard the Lord God walking about in the garden. So they hid from the Lord God among the trees. Then the Lord God called to the man, "Where are you?"

He replied, "I heard you walking in the garden, so I hid. I was afraid because I was naked."

"Who told you that you were naked?" the Lord God asked. "Have you eaten from the tree whose fruit I commanded you not to eat?"

The man replied, "It was the woman you gave me who gave me the fruit, and I ate it."

Then the Lord God asked the woman, "What have you done?"

"The serpent deceived me," she replied. "That's why I ate it."

Genesis 3:8–13

Once used to declare praise and enjoy fellowship with God and each another, Adam and Eve's words are now used to hide, self-protect, blame, evade, and justify. Words once sweet and full of life are now bitter and reek of death. This kind of speech wasn't an isolated incident ending in the garden. Instead, it became the natural tongue of all humanity. We bear the image of our first mother and father. Men and women, created to reflect the image of God and speak in ways

WORDS

ARE NOT

NEUTRAL.

that reflect his character and produce life, now also have tongues that reflect Satan, with the propensity to produce death and destruction.

Words didn't cease to be powerful or productive in the garden as a result of the fall—*they just began to produce another kind of fruit.* The book of Proverbs tell us the fruit of the tongue is either death or life (Proverbs 18:21). The words of the godly are a life-giving fountain (10:11). They encourage many (10:21) and deflect anger (15:1); but the words of the ungodly bring ruin, destroy friends (11:9), and incite anger (15:1).

WORDS OF LIFE AND DEATH

The Bible, from beginning to end, paints a robust picture of the kind of words that produce life and the kind that produce death. Proverbs is loaded with verses regarding the fruit of constructive and destructive words. The book of James gives a lengthy discourse on the power of the tongue. And most of the apostle Paul's letters reference patterns of speech, such as lying and slander, that are no longer appropriate for those who have been adopted into the family of God, as well as how members of the body of Christ should rightly relate to one another.

Many stories throughout Scripture illustrate the destructive power of the tongue. There's the familiar tale of Samson and Delilah in Judges 16, in which Delilah tormented Samson with her *nagging* day after day. In Numbers 12, Miriam and Aaron *criticized* and *conspired* against Moses. King David's wife, Michal, despised and *chastised* her husband like a child for his foolishness after seeing him dancing before the Lord (2 Samuel 6). In 1 Samuel 1, Peninnah *taunted* and *made fun of* Hannah for not being able to have children. In almost every instance, words produced a negative effect. Samson was tormented; Miriam and Aaron created division and strife which led Israel astray; Hannah became so full of despair and shame she stopped eating.

But Scripture doesn't just show us that words are destructive; it also shows they are constructive and life-giving. In 1 Samuel 25, when David determined to kill Nabal, Abigail appealed to David by reminding him of who God had created him to be and of God's mission. As a result David spared Nabal's life. In the book of Esther, Queen Esther appealed to the king on behalf of the Israelites and thwarted Haman's plan to murder Mordecai and destroy the Jewish people. And in Acts 2, Peter boldly preached the gospel to the crowd and his words "pierced their hearts," resulting in around 3,000 new believers. In each of these instances, the words spoken produced life. For David and Esther, physical life was a result, whereas Peter's words produced spiritual life in his listeners.

When I think about the power of words to produce life, I think about a friend of mine who is a gifted encourager. I received a much needed and well-timed letter from her during a season of weariness and frustration. The letter was filled with words of encouragement—words founded in Scripture, words that encouraged me to press on in faith, and words that led me to rejoice in the works of the Lord. Her words were weighty and powerful. I felt their impact immediately. It's almost as if I had been holding my breath for weeks and on reading her letter, I finally let fresh air inside my lungs. She breathed new life into me.

Words are indeed powerful. I don't think many of us would question that fact. It's likely we've seen words used in both helpful and hurtful ways. It is equally likely we've used our words in both these ways as well. So while we know the power of the tongue, and cringe when thinking back on some of the things we've said, we all still struggle to use our words to bring life rather than death.

Scripture is clear: *words are not neutral*; they are either godly or they are wicked. They will either reflect the life-giving power and blessing of God, or the death and destruction of Satan. Our words are powerful because we were created in the image of God, the author of words. He entrusted us with the gift of words, which are meant to be a reflection of him—bringing peace, harmony, unity, and life. Our words can either help us fulfill our calling as *ezers* by bringing strength to others, or they can hinder us. Because of the curse of sin, our words now also reflect those of Satan—bringing disruption, confusion, division, and destruction. We cannot escape this truth: *the words we speak either reflect God or they reflect Satan.* We can tell their source by the fruit they produce.

Questions for Reflection

The chart below shows us a distinct difference between the life-giving words of God and the destructive words of Satan.

Think about your relationships and interactions this week. Take a few moments to reflect on the words you've spoken. What adjectives would you use to describe your words? Fill your answers in the chart below. Then compare them to God's words and Satan's words.

GOD'S WORDS	SATAN'S WORDS	MY WORDS
Instruct in truth	Mislead	
Protect	Deflate	
Encourage	Discourage	
Comfort	Accuse	
Strengthen/Nourish	Demean	
Convict	Condemn	
Expose	Deceive	
Promote Peace	Divide	
Restore	Ruin	

1. Look back at the chart. What do you notice? Be prepared to share any observations you have with your group.

2. Ask a close friend what they observe about the nature of your speech. How has your speech been encouraging and life-giving, and how has it been destructive?

3. Think about some of the relationships in your life (friends, in-laws, spouse, children, co-workers, neighbors). Are they marked by strife and division, or peace and unity? How has your speech contributed?

04

THE FRUIT OF OUR WORDS

Words kill, words give life; they're either poison or fruit—
you choose.

Proverbs 18:21 MSG

As I write this book on words, the silly childhood song, "Sticks and stones may break my bones, but words can never hurt me" is echoing in my head. Or the equally popular, "I'm rubber; you're glue. Whatever you say bounces off me and sticks to you." These sing-song phrases are often the effort of a child to self-protect and deflect the hurtful words of another. But as cutesy as these phrases are, they simply aren't true. Words do hurt. They hurt because they are effective. They hurt because they are loaded with meaning. They hurt because they are powerful. Maybe a more accurate statement would be, *"Sticks and stones may break my bones, but words can win or wound me."* [1]

Besides Proverbs, I am not sure any book of the Bible devotes as much time and energy to our speech as the book of James. James understood that speech is a key indicator of spiritual maturity. He believed the surest evidence, or fruit, of our faith is not public worship, how often we read the Bible, or proficient knowledge of Scripture; the fruit of our faith and spiritual maturity is seen in our deeds and how we treat one another. This includes what we say, how we say it (including tone of voice), and why we say it. This is why James went to great lengths to warn believers about various sins such as partiality and favoritism (James 2); not showing mercy to one another (2); not caring for the widow, the orphan, and the needy (2); destructive speech (3); and selfishness and jealousy toward one another (4).

James understood the importance of the tongue's role in the life of a believer, which is why he spent an inordinate amount of time addressing it within his short letter. Throughout his entire letter, he focuses on speech, saying: we should be quick to hear, slow to speak, and slow to anger (1:19); we should speak and act as those who have been freed from sin by Christ (2:12); the tongue is powerful and destructive (3); our passions war within us and produce quarreling and boasting (4:1); and we should stop grumbling against one another (5:9).

In chapter 3, James gives us insight into the fruit that comes from wisdom, and the corruption that is rooted in our own folly:

> If you are wise and understand God's ways, prove it by living an honorable life, doing good works with the humility that comes from wisdom. But if you are bitterly jealous and there is selfish ambition in your heart, don't cover up the truth with boasting and lying. For jealousy and selfishness are not God's kind of wisdom. Such things are earthly, unspiritual, and demonic. For wherever there is jealousy and selfish ambition, there you will find disorder and evil of every kind.
>
> But the wisdom from above is first of all pure. It is also peace loving, gentle at all times, and willing to yield to others. It is full of mercy and the fruit of good deeds. It shows no favoritism and is always sincere. And those who are peacemakers will plant seeds of peace and reap a harvest of righteousness.
>
> James 3:13–18

In short, James explains a life marked by wisdom isn't boastful or dishonest or jealous or selfishly ambitious. Instead, it is pure, peace-loving, gentle, submissive, merciful, sincere, shows no favoritism, humble, content, and works to establish peace in the world. This kind of life produces an abundance of fruit. This is the surest evidence of a heart of faith. Notice the work God does in us is a result of our faith and displayed through our obedience.

God has entrusted every woman with the ability to bring strength to the relationships in her life. When we align ourselves with who God is and what he is doing in the world, he will also use us to be sources of wisdom, truth, strength, and life to those he has entrusted to us. In fact, he created us for this very purpose.

The book of Proverbs paints portraits of four women: two that bring life and two that bring death. Lady Wisdom and the wife of noble character (the Proverbs 31 woman) bring life and blessing to those around them; whereas, Lady Folly and the adulterous woman bring death and destruction.

Let's take a closer look to see how wisdom and folly display themselves through the fruit of our words.

LADY WISDOM

Over the years I've heard many women remark they need to stop talking altogether. But this is not the answer to our problem with words; refraining from speaking can be just as harmful as speaking too much or speaking in hurtful ways. God gave us the ability to speak for a reason—we have work to do. God has given us a mission—to labor alongside him in bringing aid to those in need, bettering their lives so they flourish and become more of who God created them to be and accomplish what he wants them to. God created us to reflect this aspect of his nature, and he gave us the Holy Spirit who dwells in and intends to speak through us for the good of the world, the church, and the people in our lives. *The problem isn't that we speak; the problem is what we speak, why we speak it, and how we speak it.*

This life isn't about us. It isn't about realizing our own dreams and desires. It isn't about living for ourselves. We were created to breathe life and strength into others through our interactions, which includes the words we speak to them. But if we hope to fulfill God's calling in our lives, we need wisdom. It's noteworthy that the Proverbs personify wisdom as a woman. Wisdom is essential to life—helping you understand what is right, just, and fair; guiding your actions; protecting you and providing you with refuge. With this in view, it makes complete sense that the author of Proverbs says wisdom and understanding are a blessing upon whomever they fall. Her riches transcend anything we could imagine—producing life, peace, and blessing to all who will receive her (Proverbs 3:13–18).

But wisdom is not passive, or silent, or self-protective. *Wisdom speaks.* She calls out; she cries aloud. She raises her voice beckoning others to come to her to find life, strength, understanding, and nourishment (Proverbs 1:20–22, 33; 9:3–6).

> Listen to me! For I have important things to *tell* you.
>> Everything I *say* is right,
> for I *speak* the truth
>> and detest every kind of deception.
> My *advice* is wholesome.
>> There is nothing devious or crooked in it.
> My *words* are plain to anyone with understanding,
>> clear to those with knowledge.
> Choose my *instruction* rather than silver,
>> and knowledge rather than pure gold.
> For wisdom is far more valuable than rubies.
>> Nothing you desire can compare with it.
> I, Wisdom, live together with good judgment.
>> I know where to discover knowledge and discernment.

WHEN WE ALIGN OURSELVES

WITH WHO GOD IS AND WHAT

HE IS DOING IN THE WORLD,

HE WILL ALSO USE US TO BE

SOURCES OF WISDOM, TRUTH,

STRENGTH, AND LIFE TO THOSE

HE HAS ENTRUSTED TO US.

All who fear the Lord will hate evil.
Therefore, I hate pride and arrogance,
    corruption and perverse speech.
Common sense and success belong to me.
    Insight and strength are mine.
Because of me, kings reign,
    and rulers make just decrees.
Rulers lead with my help,
    and nobles make righteous judgments.
I love all who love me.
    Those who search will surely find me.
I have riches and honor,
    as well as enduring wealth and justice.
My gifts are better than gold, even the purest gold,
    my wages better than sterling silver!
I walk in righteousness,
    in paths of justice.
Those who love me inherit wealth.
    I will fill their treasuries.

Proverbs 8:6–21 (emphasis author's own)

Wisdom speaks. But when she speaks it is for the benefit of others, not for selfish gain or vainglory. When she speaks, her words are wise, and she gives instructions with kindness (Proverbs 31:26). Wisdom speaks noble things, things that are excellent and true. Wise words will be filled with justice, righteousness, truth, discretion, understanding, wise counsel, and good judgment. Insight and strength are inherent to wisdom. Solomon compares the words of the wise to cattle prods, painful but helpful in guiding in the ways of righteousness, faithfulness, and obedience (Ecclesiastes 12:11). Teaching, instructing, and correcting in ways that produce blessing and life are characteristic of those who speak with wisdom (Proverbs 9:8–9).

As women created in the image of God and entrusted with attributes of his nature, we can speak words of wisdom—words that are constructive and life-giving. Scripture gives many examples of wise speech, some of which we can find in the list below. *As you read, pick out two or three ways in which your speech exhibits this kind of fruit.*

WORDS OF THE WISE:

- **Teach** — impart knowledge or understanding
- **Comfort** — give strength or hope to
- **Inspire/Motivate** — spur on, to infuse life
- **Heal** — restore to health, help overcome an unfavorable condition
- **Unify** — speak words that bring together or produce harmony
- **Correct** — make true or accurate, point out errors in order to improve
- **Console** — ease the grief or trouble of another
- **Guide** — lead or help direct in the path of truth
- **Encourage/Embolden** — fill with courage or strength of purpose
- **Ennoble** — elevate another in excellence, dignity or respect
- **Edify** — speak words that build up, not in a way that puffs up or flatters but strengthens; promotes growth in Christian obedience, faithfulness, and maturity
- **Admonish/Exhort** — warn, urge, reprove gently
- **Helpful/Beneficial** — speak what aids, assists, supports; speak words that are of use or benefit, produce good effects
- **Necessary** — speak what is essential, needed, crucial
- **Bless** — speak well of, praise, celebrate

There is no wickedness, corruption, deception, pride, perverseness, or arrogance to be found in wise speech. Wisdom doesn't speak in ways that are vague and difficult for people to decipher, but plain and clear. In essence this means saying what we mean and meaning what we say. So when your husband or someone else asks you if something is wrong, you don't say, "Nothing," when clearly something is wrong. It also means you don't beat around the bush or drop hints, expecting others to understand something you've never clearly spoken, and then punishing them when they don't.

Ultimately, wisdom is characteristic of the Lord himself. If we are to speak with wisdom in a way the benefits the world around us, we must seek the Lord, who is generous and will give wisdom to all who ask (Proverbs 2:6a; James 1:5). True wisdom comes from him. If we want to be women who speak with wisdom (Proverbs 31:26), then we must call out to Jesus, who is the wisdom of God in the flesh (1 Corinthians 1:24, 30). Jesus is the Word of God, the power of God, and the true wisdom of God. We must ask him to inhabit our lives, our words, and our relationships. We must seek him so that we will more accurately reflect his character, that the words flowing from our mouths will be full of his wisdom, life, and truth. When we allow Jesus to transform us from the inside out, others will be blessed by the words we speak and find strength and life in our presence.

LADY FOLLY

Solomon says that a wise woman builds her house, but folly tears it down with her own hands (Proverbs 14:1). Just as Solomon personifies wisdom as a woman, he also personifies folly as a woman. Lady Folly is loud, brash, and abrasive (Proverbs 9:13). She speaks out of her own ignorance and lack of understanding (Proverbs 9:13). She elevates herself and meddles in the lives of others, who are minding their own business (Proverbs 9:14-15). Folly is foolishness; it is speech that lacks substance and nourishment to enrich the lives of others. Folly at worst leads others astray, and at best leaves them wandering blindly in the dark on their own. Whereas Lady Wisdom benefits those around her, Lady Folly benefits no one—not even herself.

The adulterous woman to whom Solomon often refers is also, like Lady Folly, characterized by her speech, which is smooth, seductive, and persuasive. Her paths lead to death, destruction, and chaos. Smooth speech sounds good. It is a delight to our ears, often telling us what we want to hear rather than what we need to hear. Smooth speech in the form of flattery is often deceptive and self-centered. We use it to win others over—whether out of self-protective fear or self-promoting desires for selfish gain—to attach them to ourselves rather than pointing them to God.

Lest I think I can distance myself from the attributes of Lady Folly or the adulterous woman, Proverbs has one more example which I simply can't ignore—the quarrelsome, nagging, fretful and contentious wife, which is mentioned not just once, but four times. The language the writer uses conjures palpable images, comparing her to a constant dripping, and everyone knows how annoying that can be! So annoying, in fact, he says it would be better to live in the desert or on the corner of a rooftop than to be in her presence (Proverbs 21:9; 21:19; 25:24; 27:15).

Think about how children use nagging to wear you down when they want something. It drains your energy, and it's easy to give into their desires just for a moment of peace. A wife has the God-given capacity to be a source of respite, refuge, and life for those in her household, but because she is prone to nag and quarrel and fret, she becomes someone her husband runs from rather than someone he runs to in order to find respite. But this doesn't just happen in a husband-and-wife relationship. We use our words in contentious, quarrelsome, and nagging ways with our friends, co-workers, in-laws, and employers. We may do it with constant questioning, making others justify and explain themselves to us. We might do it through belaboring points in an argument to get others to concede to us and our desires. However we go about it,

OUR WORDS,

INSTEAD OF BEING TOOLS

THROUGH WHICH WE LIVE

OUT GOD'S CALLING, BECOME

OBSTACLES THAT HINDER

US FROM BEING HELPFUL

OR WEAPONS THAT BRING

DESTRUCTION TO THOSE

AROUND US.

the results are the same. *Rather than being a source of strength and life to others, we drain them of it.* The unfortunate truth is that my words aren't always used in ways that bring strength or life to others. I can't help but think about how often I use my words to correct my husband, as if he were a child. Or how many times I question him or repeatedly remind him. I think about how I use sarcasm or slander as a self-protective layer around my heart to guard it from the barbed words of others. Instead of speaking words of wisdom, truth, and encouragement, I find myself speaking words of criticism and judgment and disapproval. Whether directly or indirectly, I use my words to distance myself from others, not wanting to identify with them. Or I use my words to point out others' flaws and weaknesses in ways that are not fruitful or constructive.

On any given day, this is true of all of us in varying degrees. Rather than using our words to build others up, we use them to tear others down. We speak in ways that demean, marginalize, and invalidate. We dismiss, humiliate, and embarrass—sometimes in obvious ways, and other times through more subtle, passive-aggressive ways like sarcasm. Instead of bringing strength to others, we deflate them. Instead of being a source of refuge and respite, we become someone from whom they must protect themselves. Our words, instead of being tools through which we live out God's calling, become obstacles that hinder us from being helpful or weapons that bring destruction to those around us.

Our speech exhibits that of Lady Folly or the adulteress woman in many ways, all of which are destructive. Throughout Scripture, various corruptions of the tongue are highlighted, many listed below. *As you read, pick out three or four words that are characteristic of the struggles you have.*

WORDS OF THE FOOLISH:

- **Gossip** — unconstrained talk about others (typically marked by unconfirmed or untrue details)

- **Slander** — make false and damaging statements to smear someone's character
- **Scorn** — harbor contempt (says others are worthless)
- **Mock** — contempt-fueled belittling (typically includes laughing at)
- **Scoff** — speak to someone about something in a scornful/mocking way
- **Quarrelsome/contentious/argumentative** — a perpetually combative posture
- **Strife** — bitter disagreement/conflict
- **Lie** — say or withhold something with the intent to deceive someone who has the right to know the truth
- **Manipulate** — influence others in an exploitive, self-serving way
- **Boast** — self-praise
- **Curse** — wish harm/injury upon someone
- **Insult/criticize** — search for and magnify fault in others
- **Insolent** — show haughtiness, lack of respect for others or authority
- **Foul/rotten/unwholesome/perverse speech** — deliberately toxic or degrading
- **Harsh** — cruel and severe language, abrasive
- **Abusive** — excessive and repeatedly cruel and severe language
- **Grumble/discontent** — always finding fault, complaining or expressing ingratitude
- **Promise-breaking** — retract/undercut a once-given assurance
- **Flatter** — excessive and/or insincere praise for the purpose of endearing someone to yourself, manipulation

- **Busybody/meddle** — interfere with others' affairs; treating what should be merely a concern as if it's your responsibility
- **Stir up division** — promote disunity & hostility among people; causing disagreement between people, which leads to separation; creating disharmony
- **Nag** — find fault incessantly; to annoy someone with repeated requests, questions, or orders; to badger someone
- **Careless speech** — thoughtless, unprofitable, lazy speech, injurious, tactless, curt, blunt, or "matter-of-fact"
- **Distance oneself** — separate oneself from others, usually from a position of self-righteousness and judgment, often marked by using the word "they" (e.g. "I don't know why *they* did that!" Or, "What are *they* thinking?!")
- **Withhold truth** — to not speak into a situation or someone else's life for fear of retribution, being misunderstood, being wrong, risking the relationship; or due to choosing one's own comfort over the other person (inconvenience, lack of interest, etc.)

When we look at a list like this, it's tempting to become discouraged. Your discouragement will either compel you to work harder to fix it on our own or drive you into despair and self-contempt. Neither of these will produce the type of fruit that comes through faith. You can't staple good fruit to a bad tree, nor can you pluck bad fruit from a bad tree and expect it to not continue to produce. We must address the root.

Questions for Reflection

1. As you looked at the two lists, Words of the Wise and Words of the Foolish, which descriptions did you feel were most accurate of your speech?

2. As you think back over conversations you've had this past week, think about how they impacted others. Circle the words that best describe the fruit of those conversations.

Empowering	Healing	Thoughtful	Resentful
Discouraging	Worrisome	Emotional	Distancing
Frustrating	Challenging	Painful	Embarrassing
Strengthening	Hurtful	Scrutinizing	Affirming
Peaceful	Helpful	Chastising	Flattering
Calming	Divisive	Belittling	Wholesome
Angering	Insightful	Encouraging	Maturing

3. As you look at the words you circled, what do you learn about yourself? How does it make you feel?

05

THE ROOT OF OUR WORDS

What you say flows from what is in your heart.

Luke 6:45

I remember it like it was yesterday. On June 17, 2015, nine men and women were gunned down by a stranger they had welcomed into their church during a Bible study. It was a senseless act of hatred and bigotry. They opened their lives to a man who betrayed their kindness and love in the worst possible way. At a time when other cities had given way to riots and violence in the face of injustice, the whole country watched and waited to see how the city of Charleston and the members of Mother Emanuel AME church would respond. I watched the ongoing news footage in awe. The family members of those killed didn't blame politicians or policies. They didn't rant or rage. They didn't lash out. They didn't seek pity or power. Instead, they filled the street singing hymns of thanksgiving and praise to God. I will never forget listening to the church members and people of Charleston who had gathered in front of the church singing, "How Great Thou Art," just days after they had lost their pastor, friends, mothers, fathers, sisters, and brothers. The families of those killed expressed deep anguish and hurt, and yet extended forgiveness and unmerited grace to the man who had taken from them. Their words didn't incite division and discord in the community; instead they inspired unity and peace. Their response caused me to think about injustices, how I've been wounded in far less tragic ways and yet have withheld love, forgiveness, and mercy. Do I respond in a way that produces division and discord in my community, or unity and peace? In the midst of their darkest hour, they were a beacon of light. This tiny little church outshone even the sun in all its magnificence. They had been cut to the quick, and yet they bled grace, peace, and praise.

Missionary Amy Carmichael once said that "a cup brimful of sweetness cannot spill even one drop of bitter water, no matter how suddenly jarred." [1] This statement is profound and true. The circumstances of life have a way of revealing what's really on the inside of a person. The words of praise and forgiveness flowing from the men and women of Mother Emanuel reflected hearts that knew and loved Jesus, hearts surrendered to his plan even when they couldn't possibly understand what he was doing.

On the flip side, I've heard women (and men) dismiss their own words as uncharacteristic. "I didn't mean that. I was just tired." Or "I never would have said that if you hadn't . . ." Or "I don't know why I said that; that's not me." But, according to Jesus, we cannot divorce ourselves from the words we speak.

> A good tree can't produce bad fruit, and a bad tree can't produce good fruit. A tree is identified by its fruit. Figs are never gathered from thornbushes, and grapes are not picked from bramble bushes. A good person produces good things from the treasury of a good heart, and an evil person produces evil things from the treasury of an evil heart. What you say flows from what is in your heart.

Luke 6:43–45

Before gossip leaves your lips, it begins in your heart. Before angry, dishonest, or quarrelsome words form on your tongue, they form in your heart. *The fruit is native to the tree. It matches.* If there is anger in the heart, there is anger on the tree. If there is lying on the tree, there is dishonesty and deceitfulness in the heart. A heart rooted in thanksgiving can't produce words of discontentment and grumbling. Likewise, a heart rooted in God's grace and mercy can't produce words that are vengeful and bitter. If your words are prickly or thorny, the problem is your heart—not the person or circumstance. Circumstances only reveal what is in your heart. A sick tree is going to produce sick fruit, or no fruit at all. A healthy tree will produce healthy fruit. *Just as fruit is native to the tree, words are native to the heart.*

This indictment of the heart can be difficult to bear. What does this mean about who you are as a person and as a Christian? That's a valid question and one not to be dismissed. To explore the depths of the human heart is a risky journey—one requiring humility and openness as well as a resolute confidence in Jesus as the solution to our sin and depravity. Many would rather remain blissfully ignorant. But this is fertile ground where good work can be done in the believer's heart. This kind of heart work is crucial in the life of a Christian:

> This is the message we heard from Jesus and now declare to you: God is light, and there is no darkness in him at all. So we are lying if we say we have fellowship with God but go on living in spiritual darkness; we are not practicing the truth. But if we are living in the light, as God is in the light, then we have fellowship with each other, and the blood of Jesus, his Son, cleanses us from all sin.
>
> If we claim we have no sin, we are only fooling ourselves and not living in the truth. But if we confess our sins to him, he is faithful and just to forgive us our sins and to cleanse us from all wickedness. If we claim we have not sinned, we are

calling God a liar and showing that his word has no place in our hearts.

1 John 1:5–10

We cannot have fellowship with God and continue to live in spiritual darkness. We need to bring the darkness of our hearts into the light. We are more comfortable talking about sin in our past, but it is much more challenging to confess current sin in our lives. Ironically this is the first step toward finding freedom. Sin grows in the dark, but dies in the light of exposure. So, with faith and courage, we must explore the depths of our hearts and bring what we find into the light of day.

God uses all kinds of vehicles to deliver his spiritual truth, one of which I found in an unlikely place—Jim Collins' business book *Good to Great*. As I read, I couldn't help but notice the parallel between the Christian life and the companies Collins said made the leap from good to great. After five years of research, Collins discovered the good-to-great companies displayed distinctive forms of disciplined thought, such as being committed to confronting the brutal facts of reality. Collins stated that when "you start with an honest and diligent effort to determine the truth of the situation, the right decisions often become self-evident . . . and even if all decisions do not become self-evident, one thing is certain: You absolutely cannot make a series of good decisions without first confronting the brutal facts." [2]

This kind of disciplined thought is just as important, if not more so, for us as followers of Jesus. The Bible warns us to "guard our hearts above all else because it determines the course of our lives" (Proverbs 4:23). Self-awareness is a valuable commodity both in business and in the lives of believers. And it is a discipline we must cultivate if we desire to gain ground in the battle of the tongue. *Our hearts will determine the course of our words.*

Confronting the brutal facts of reality is a crucial part of cultivating self-awareness. One good-to-great executive said it's equivalent to turning over rocks and looking at what's beneath. He said, "When you

JUST AS FRUIT

IS NATIVE TO THE TREE,

WORDS ARE NATIVE TO

THE HEART.

turn over rocks and look at all the squiggly things underneath, you can either put the rock down, or you can say, 'My job is to turn over the rocks and look at the squiggly things,' even if what you see can scare [you]." [3] Like this executive, we can turn over the rocks of our words, look at the squiggly things underneath, and put them back down in denial. Or we can turn them over and allow God, in his mercy, to expose us, call us out of shame and hiding, and bring us into the light of his freedom, power, mercy, and grace.

This is a discipline that can be learned, but requires creating margin in our lives, investing time and energy into self-examination, engaging in authentic community with others, and a humble openness to what the Lord chooses to reveal about ourselves. It is never fun to come face-to-face with our sin. In fact, it's rather painful to be confronted with the harsh reality of the wickedness still at work within our own hearts. It's easy to become weary and weighed down with shame and despair. If these feelings aren't dealt with properly, they may, like Adam and Eve, lure us into hiding, covering, and blame shifting. But we must do the hard work to come into the light and excavate our hearts to uncover the squiggly things beneath the words we speak, because "what comes out of our mouths is usually an accurate index of the health of our hearts." [4]

THE DISEASED HEART

WEAKNESS

Many aspects impact the health of our hearts, two of which are *weakness* and *idolatry*. A key principle in recovery from substance addiction is HALT. The idea behind the acronym is an addict or alcoholic is more tempted to use when they are hungry, angry, lonely, or tired. The recovery community recognizes frailties of the body can lead to harmful responses. The same is true with our words. Jesus said the spirit is willing, but the body is weak (Matthew 26:41). In moments of weakness, we have less self-restraint, less self-control. We are particularly weak and vulnerable when our bodies are hungry, weary, sick, or in pain. But we are also weak and vulnerable when we are afraid, hurt, grieving, anxious, or under emotional stress. This weakness often leaves us vulnerable to the body's natural impulses, which creates opportunities for sinful responses.

If you are like me, you are more prone to snappy or prickly responses when you are tired or hungry. Likewise, when we are afraid or hurt, we are more tempted toward being self-protective, withdrawn, and unapproachable. Our responses are not *because* we are tired or hungry or afraid; our responses are because of our *hearts*. The weakness of our body only allows room for what's in our hearts to spill out of our mouths.

Personally, my words have revealed my own frailty and fragility. Early on in our marriage, my husband took me on an epic adventure to the Grand Canyon. We were to hike forty miles over four days on a less traveled trail. I was nervous months before the trip even happened. That anxiety often gave way to agitation, tense conversations, and persistent questioning, all of which exhibited my lack of trust in him and in his planning. But the tension reached its climax on the third day as we hiked along a narrow cliff ledge, which at times was only wide enough to place one foot in front of the other. I was terrified to say the least. And the more scared I got, the angrier I got.

I fought back tears for three grueling miles as we skirted the cliff's edge, while my husband skipped along behind me, clueless to the fury brewing in my heart. I found myself reciting portions of Psalm 139 in an attempt to calm my anxious heart, "Lord, you know when I sit down or when I stand up . . . You see me when I travel and when I rest at home . . . You go before me and follow me . . . Every day of my life was recorded in your book. Every moment was laid out before a single day had passed."

No matter how hard I tried, I could not calm my anxious heart. Terror gripped me. I was hyper aware of my weakness, frailty, and vulnerability. But my husband, unaware of my struggle, was singing worship music at the top of his lungs, having the time of his life. As my anger grew, I began to curse him under my breath, until I finally blurted, "Will you shut up!" I wish I could say that was the extent of my outburst, but it got worse. When we finally reached the end of the narrow trail and found more spacious paths, all the emotions I had been holding back finally erupted. While my husband and his brother explored an outcropping overlooking the Colorado River below, I spewed angry, hateful venom to my sister-in-law—calling my husband immature, an idiot, and a few other choice words.

Just moments before I had been reciting portions of God's word, but now I was cursing my joy-filled husband. Just as James said, sometimes the tongue praises our Lord and Father, and sometimes it curses those who have been made in his image (James 3:9). In that moment of weakness and vulnerability, both blessing and cursing poured from my mouth (James 3:10). But I couldn't blame my reaction on my circumstances, my fear, or my husband. As James goes on to say, *it is impossible for a fig tree to produce olives or a grapevine to produce figs, and it is impossible to draw fresh water from a salty spring* (James 3:11). And boy was my spring salty! The fruit of my mouth, in my moment of weakness, was consistent with what was in my heart.

This doesn't mean we will never respond well in moments of weakness or frailty. On the contrary, I've witnessed remarkable displays of faith from people in the bitterest of circumstances. A friend of mine has experienced years of heartbreak over infertility and miscarriage, and still uses her words to declare the faithfulness of God. She doesn't deny her pain and loss, but the words she uses to express her grief are evidence of a heart surrendered to the Lord. Another friend has been terribly mistreated by a family member for several years. Whenever she discusses the situation with me, she uses words that confer dignity and respect to the person who has hurt her deeply. And as weary and worn as she is from the situation, her words are always measured and carefully chosen. The words these women use in the midst of their circumstances indicate hearts deeply rooted in Jesus.

Question for Reflection

1. When are you the weakest and most vulnerable to the sins of the tongue? Is it when you are physically tired, in pain, sick, or hungry? Is it at the end of a long day of work? How does that affect your speech? How can being aware of your weaknesses help you?

IDOLATRY

A second factor that impacts the health of our heart is idolatry. Idolatry is when good desires become ultimate desires. Idols often take root wherever there is a gap of faith—where we struggle to believe God is enough. When these desires begin to rule over us, we're deceived into thinking we must have them. Then, because of our autonomy, we do whatever it takes to fulfill them. After his long indictment of the tongue, James points his readers to the heart of the problem, "What is causing the quarrels and fights among you? Don't they come from the evil desires at war within you?" (James 4:1). The division, conflict, and quarreling we experience in fellowship with others often originates from our own evil desires. The idea James is conveying is that of passions, things we desire or crave. All of us have passions and desires. *It's when those desires go awry—when they displace your love for God and others—that they become evil.* Those exact passions and desires are often at the root of the division and conflict we have with one another.

I love and desire order in my home. Maybe you can relate? I don't necessarily need the house to be clean, but I want everything to be in its proper place. To me, home is refuge—a place of safety and rest. So when there is disorder, I can't rest. Disarray and clutter in my house gives rise to anxiety and that anxiety produces frustration. This desire would often lead to conflict with my teenager, who was perfectly content to leave things wherever. Yes, he needed to be responsible, but that wasn't what drove our conflicts. The true issue resided in the fact he was in between me and my desire, which meant he was on the receiving end of my wrath until order in my world was restored. Sometimes I punished him through withdrawal and silent treatments, speaking in passive-aggressive ways, or giving short and curt responses. Other times I was much more overt—chastising instead of correcting, demeaning instead of ennobling. My desires for order displaced my love for him and it reflected in my words.

Our desires pit us against one another and cause us to strive for what we want at the cost of others. James says we pursue these desires at the expense of our neighbors, "You want what you don't have, so you scheme and kill to get it. You are jealous of what others have, but you can't get it, so you fight and wage war to take it away from them" (James 4:2). We seek retribution or justice and so we slander others and assassinate their character. We want to feel a part, so we join in or initiate gossip. We want to be right, so we discredit others and smear their reputation. We fight and wage war against others through manipulation, nagging, boasting, flattering, backbiting, gossiping, stirring up division, and fueling arguments.

SEVEN IDOLS THAT MAY BE
GOVERNING YOUR SPEECH

Here is where we need to pick up the rock and see what kinds of squiggly things are lurking underneath—the disordered passions and desires that govern our speech. Below are seven examples of corrupted desires—or idols. The list is not extensive and the way they manifest in our lives will be different according to each woman, but this list can serve as a good diagnostic tool as we seek to assess the health of our hearts. Each of these idols can produce a myriad of fruit in our lives, but for the purpose of this study we are going to examine how they impact our speech. As you read through these, pay close attention to how Christ transforms each of these desires.

COMFORT

Comfort is the desire for pleasure, convenience, and freedom from suffering or difficulty. When the desire for comfort rules a woman's life, others are often in her way. Their needs, their desires, their weaknesses and failings interfere with her desires for a life of ease, peace, and order. Rather than placing others' needs above her own, she sees them as obstacles to overcome in her pursuit of comfort. And her growing sense of entitlement leads to bitterness and resentment when her needs aren't met.

Comfort and I are well-acquainted. It's probably the biggest idol in my life and at the root of many of my relational conflicts. As an introverted comfort-addict, I have a tendency to withdraw from relationships in self-preservation. I rationalize and justify it as my natural need to recharge, which is only partly true. Sometimes I just don't want to exert the effort necessary to connect. This desire for comfort leads me to disengage when others are talking, halfway listening and offering the obligatory "hmm" or "okay" but never fully engaging in the conversation or seeing how I can invest in them at that moment.

The idol of comfort doesn't just show up in passive ways in my life. When my comfort is threatened, I can also come out swinging. This desire often created tension in my relationship with my son. I tend to have a weak immune system, so when my son would come home with the sniffles or a sore throat or the dreaded stomach bug, my compassion went out the window. All I could think was, "Great! Now I'm going to get sick." Because I saw him as a threat to my life of comfort and ease, my words were short and lacking any evidence of empathy. Instead, I barked orders—telling him to cover his mouth or pick up his tissues or whatever I viewed as his assault on my comfort in that moment.

How the idol of comfort governs a woman's speech will look different for everyone, though there may be some common tendencies:

- It's the woman who may be short, curt, and prickly, because she is inwardly resentful of those who threaten her comfort.

- It's the woman who withdraws from fellowship with her friends when things get hard, when they are suffering, or when conflict arises. She just wants friendships to be easy and fun.

- It's the woman who may get frustrated and lash out, deflecting and accusing others of not being sensitive to her needs.

- It's the woman who may disengage, not participate, or be aloof in conversations because it takes too much effort.

Ultimately, the idol of comfort is self-centered, not others-centered. Jesus didn't teach that we should seek our best life now or pursue our own comfort. Instead he reminded us suffering and sacrifice are a normal, honorable part of the Christian life. We need to remind ourselves Jesus set aside the ultimate comfort he had with the Father before the world began in order to identify with us in hardship and suffering. He rejected seeking a life of ease and chose instead to be persecuted and die a painful death on the cross for us, that we might know the comfort of his suffering. He promised that when we experience hardship, when we grieve or mourn, when we sacrifice for the gospel or for our brother and sisters in Christ, an eternal reward awaits that is far more glorious than the fleeting comforts of this life. We must preach Christ to our souls until our death-grip on comfort loosens, and we can instead surrender to God's plan. We can remind ourselves that God is the *source* of all comfort. He comforts us in all our troubles *so that* we can then comfort others with the same comfort he has given to us (2 Corinthians 1:4). With these truths in mind, we can choose to forgo the comfort of the moment. We can embrace hardship and suffering. We can overlook minor inconveniences and petty annoyances. We can see others in our lives as opportunities to invest in Christ's kingdom rather than obstacles in building our own. We can embrace sacrifice and choose to love and serve others, rather than serving ourselves. And we can do so knowing the comfort we truly desire can only be found in Christ.

GLORY

The desire for glory is based on a need for the praise, honor, and admiration of others. A woman who idolizes glory wants to be the best, prettiest, most competent, and most popular. Her desire often leads to overfunctioning and self-promotion. She may be the one who wants to throw the best parties, have the cleanest home, or wow others with the amazing food she makes. She may strive to have the best ideas at work. She's the one who comes in early and leaves late, always quick to volunteer to lead the next project. She strives to make sure her husband and children look their best and behave in a manner that reflects well on her. She prides herself on being the one people count on—someone who is always there in a pinch, always dependable and diligent. Underneath her exceptional performance is a craving for the praise and admiration of those around her. The idol of glory can lead to a sense of entitlement, anger, or bitterness when others don't praise her. She might become critical of those in her life when their behavior, appearance, or choices reflect badly on her. Ultimately at the root of the idol of glory is a desire to be worshiped.

How the corrupted desire for glory governs a woman's speech will look different for everyone, though there may be some common tendencies:

- It's the woman who believes she deserves kids who live according to her desires, or a husband who pursues her the way she thinks she should be pursued. When they don't live up to her expectations she becomes critical, bitter, and resentful. Instead of loving and speaking life into her family, she grumbles, complains, and nags.

- It's the woman who places unrealistic demands on her friends. She is always dissatisfied because they never do enough to meet her needs. Her need trumps anything that's going on in other's lives. She is an emotional bully who tries to make others cater to her.

- It's the employee who thinks she deserved the promotion more than her coworker. Instead of celebrating her coworker's accomplishment, she gossips, slanders, and discredits them to her peers. Or she criticizes her superiors—claiming favoritism or incompetence led to the decision rather than her coworker's merits.

- It's the woman who feels threatened by others' accomplishments or is jealous when others receive public praise. She finds ways to illicit praise by proving herself more capable, more desirable, more valuable.

- It's the woman who seeks to build a social media following because she craves the attention, fame, and praise the platform brings her. She orients her life around the next post, the next photo, the next video.

- It's the woman who pushes her children to succeed academically, athletically, and/or spiritually, and then extols their accomplishments in conversations with others, seeking to find glory in how her children are perceived by others.

- It's the woman who has an elevated opinion of herself and as a result often criticizes others' work, appearances, choices.

- It's the woman who has to be the best, has to one-up others. If someone tells a story, she has one that's better. If someone experienced something terrible and is getting attention from others, she tells a similar story to regain the attention.

- It's the woman who publicly expresses her opinions and sentiments to highlight her good character and moral correctness on a particular issue (virtue signaling). She aligns herself with the cause of the day, then revels in the adoring comments others post about what a good person she is.

Ultimately, the idol of glory comes from an exaggerated sense of self-importance and the expectation the world should worship you, which is contrary to Scripture. God will not share his glory with another (Isaiah 42:8). When we see this hunger for glory in the words we speak, we must remind ourselves Jesus is the only one who is truly worthy and deserving of glory. The only thing we deserve is God's wrath, judgment, and eternal damnation. But God, in his mercy, looked upon us with compassion and gave us what we didn't deserve—grace, mercy, and forgiveness. And yet, our sin and rebellion couldn't go unpunished. Jesus bore all of the judgment due us. He traded his glory for our shame. He took on the punishment he didn't deserve so we could, in turn, receive the reward we didn't deserve. Reflecting on this, preaching this truth to ourselves, should instill in our souls an attitude of humility. A spirit of humility will enable us to embrace and accept others, rather than criticize them. We can allow others to live according to what is best for them, rather than what best serves us. We are freed from the poison of bitterness and resentment over unmet expectations. We find the freedom to live in obscurity and make peace with being an average, everyday Jane. Jesus had every reason to feel entitled—he is entitled to our worship, our service, and our very lives. And yet he gave up his rights! Everything we have is solely because of God's grace; everything is a gift. When the humiliation of the cross—the knowledge that someone had to die in order for us to live—is pressed into our hearts, humility grows. This frees us from grandiose ideas of our own rights to glory, and, as a result, our words will exhibit humility, modesty, kindness, selflessness, and generosity.

JUSTICE

Justice is a desire for fairness and equitability. A desire for justice isn't bad. We can and should pursue justice for the oppressed—like the poor, widows, and orphans. This is a good, God-honoring pursuit. But this desire is corrupted and becomes an idol when we are unwilling to forgive actual or perceived injustices done to us or seek to right these wrongs on our own terms. A woman who is governed by a justice idol may consciously and willfully seek to hurt the person who hurt her. Or she may do so subconsciously, unaware of her actions or motivations. When a desire for justice is present, bitterness and resentment are not far off.

How a corrupted desire for justice governs a woman's speech will look different for everyone, though there may be some common tendencies:

- It's the wife who never allows her husband to forget about a poor decision he made years ago. She continues to remind him of his failures and their impact on her life. She not only brings it up in conversations between the two of them, she also brings it up in conversations with others, furthering his humiliation.

- It's the woman who has been the subject of gossip and slander and the unresolved sense of betrayal and hostility leads her to retaliate. She soothes her wounded heart through harsh, judgmental, critical words or sarcastic remarks.

- It's the young girl whose boyfriend broke up with her and she stirs up drama attempting to win others to her side by playing the victim. She plays on the sympathy of others, stirring them to not only feel bad for her but to also feel angry at him for hurting her.

- It's the woman who was abused by her grandfather as a young girl, and now she punishes every man she knows. She demeans and criticizes them. She treats every man as if he was her grandfather. She speaks to them and about them with contempt.

- It's the woman whose friend said something unkind to her, and she has a hard time moving past it. She is snarky, sarcastic, and curt in all of their conversations. It's easier to be angry than admit hurt, so she becomes defensive and self-protective, shutting her friend out.

- It's the woman who uses social media to vent about perceived injustices, even to the extent of posting pictures of someone who cut her off in traffic, or took up two places in a parking lot, or cut in front of her in line.

Ultimately, when justice governs our speech it stems from a lack of belief in a just God who will right all wrongs. It is also a product of our demonizing of one another. When someone hurts us, we tend to assume the worst of them. We believe their actions were careless at best or intentional at worst. We fail to remember hurt people often hurt people. God is just. Because he is just, he will address all wrongs. He cannot overlook them. Everything that has ever been done to you will be accounted for in the end. Everything. If the person who hurt you is a believer, then Jesus has already paid the price for their sin. He received their punishment. He's already made it right. You cannot continue to try to extract payment from them when its already covered. But if they are not a believer, then their sin is not yet paid for. This means when they come face-to-face with God, he will call them to account for their wrongs. Justice will be done. They will pay for how they hurt you. It's a far worse punishment to fall into the hands of a holy God, than it is to fall into the hands of a mere human being. When I think about the people who have hurt me suffering such a terrible fate, an unexpected sense of compassion wells up inside me. It frees me to forgive them. I am released from the bitterness and anger that fuels my desire for justice. Instead, I am freed to pray for them, forgive them, and love them despite how they may have wounded me—which in turn transforms my speech.

APPROVAL

The idol of approval is the longing to be accepted by others, to have them affirm your personhood and worth. This desire is often rooted in fear of man or insecurity. A woman seeking approval needs people more than she loves them, which again puts her at odds with those in her life, and she will work to attain that approval through a variety of ways. She is fragile and vulnerable because she needs others to affirm her. She desires to be seen as competent and valuable. If she feels unappreciated, she may give way to despair and self-pity. Or she may become frustrated and bitter toward those whose opinions she most values when they don't respond as she needs them to.

How the idol of approval governs a woman's speech will look different for everyone, though there may be some common tendencies:

- This is the mother of three young children who speaks about herself in self-deprecating ways, which causes others to feel the need to respond favorably and assuage her insecurities.

- It's the young woman who uses flattery or excessive compliments in attempts to win others over, especially those in positions of power and influence.

- It's the woman who withholds truth from her friend rather than confronting the wrong. She may evade, soften, or not speak the truth at all because she can't risk someone being upset with her or not liking her.

- This is the young woman who, finding herself in a new peer group, participates in gossip and slander in order to gain affirmation and secure her place in the group.

- It's the woman who is ruled and dominated by others' opinions, so she has to vindicate or prove herself when someone has an unfavorable opinion of her.

- It's the wife who is frustrated and feels devalued because her husband never compliments her. Because she needs his words of affirmation, she often nags him or tries to guilt him into praising her more. But when he does compliment her, she tells him it doesn't count since he's just doing it because she asked him to.

- It's the woman who frequently seeks affirmation through her social media posts and engagement, always posting flattering pictures of herself.

Ultimately, the idol of approval is rooted in the fear of man. "We fear people because they can expose and humiliate us. We fear people because they can reject, ridicule, or despise us. We fear people because they can attack, oppress, or threaten us." [5] This is a dangerous place to find ourselves, because it will govern our words as well as our actions. When we fear people, we are dependent on them to make us okay. We need them to validate us, to provide us with security in our personhood. But Scripture tells us it's never safe to base our identity and worth on the fickle opinions of sinful humanity rather than the stable truth of God's word. Needing approval can lead us to make concessions where we shouldn't, to not speak truth when we should. It's like drinking water from a broken cistern. There is no nourishment or satisfaction to be found. Compliments last mere moments and then they fade away. But who you are in Christ is secure for all eternity. God has adopted you into his family as his beloved daughter and declared you righteous, holy, without accusation, without condemnation, without blemish or fault. You are already deeply loved, fully pleasing, totally forgiven, accepted and complete in Christ. This is a more real, more substantial truth about yourself than anyone else's perceptions or opinions. When you are no longer governed by your need for others' affirmation and approval, you are free to love them without constraint, which will shape and govern the way you communicate with them. You will no longer be frustrated by their failure to affirm you because you have all of the acceptance you need. You will be able to speak grace and truth into the lives of those around you without fear. Rather than needing them, feeding from them, and thereby draining them of strength, you will be able to more fully live your calling as an *ezer*—becoming a source of life and speaking in ways that foster strength and growth.

CONTROL

Control is the corrupted desire to direct or manage life and people according to what you believe is best. A woman who is ruled by the idol of control must have everything in life go according to her plan. She may be risk-averse and does not like being placed in positions of vulnerability. She often requires assurances, certainty, and clarity from those around her. Those in relationship with her often feel like they have to prove themselves to her before she is willing to support them. Because others feel dominated by her they either become hostile and push back, or they withdraw in self-protection. They may also feel condemned or judged—like they can never do anything right or meet her standards. She operates from a belief she is right, and that others need to meet or conform to her needs, demands, ideals, or standards, producing quarreling, strife, and discord in some of her closest relationships.

How the idol of control governs a woman's speech will look different for everyone, though there may be some common tendencies:

- It's the woman who continues to meddle in her adult children's lives. She feels the need to help them succeed, offering unsolicited advice on everything from finances to parenting.

- It's the woman who is critical and condemning of how other people live their lives because she thinks she knows best. Though she is often critical of others, she is unable to receive criticism without becoming hypersensitive or defensive.

- It's the woman whose husband lost his job and she badgers him regarding the future. Rather than sacrificing her right to be afraid in order to encourage and be a source of strength for him, she is ruled by fear and her need for assurances.

- It's the woman who can't handle ambiguity and asks a thousand questions—which are less about what she needs to know in order to be helpful and more about her lack of trust and unwillingness to be vulnerable.

- It's the woman who tends to correct others in conversations. She may tell others how to drive or how to do their jobs. This may be the mom who gets her child to do the laundry or load the dishwasher but then hovers over their shoulder, telling them how to do it, or she chides them for not doing it right, and then goes back behind them and does it herself.

- It's the woman who is sometimes called bossy or intimidating. Her direct communication style, which she often admires in herself, leaves others guarded or wounded.

- It's the woman who needs to be right or win. She tends to dismiss others in conversations or she invalidates their thoughts, opinions, or feelings.

- It's the grandmother who manipulates her children through guilt trips, saying things like, "I never see you anymore" or "The grandkids are going to forget who I am." Her hints are passive-aggressive expressions of her displeasure with her children's lack of availability, and her attempts to get them to do what she wants without directly asking for it.

- It's the woman who tries to manage her image or the image of her family through evasive and/or superficial conversations and filtered social media posts.

IF WE HOPE TO GAIN

GROUND IN THE BATTLE

WITH OUR TONGUES, WE MUST

ENTRUST EVERYTHING TO GOD'S

CAPABLE, LOVING HANDS.

Interestingly enough, because words are tools, many of our conversational tendencies point to our deep-seated need for control. We use our words in order to get what we want. We may want to elicit a certain response from someone; we may be trying to steer others toward our way of thinking, to convince them of our rightness; or we may use our words to get others to act in a way we want. However it manifests in our lives, I believe most of us are governed by this corrupted desire in varying ways and degrees. Ultimately, this stems from a need for assurances and certainty. Rather than trusting God, we trust ourselves. We act autonomously, seeking to establish security and control circumstances through our own means, rather than in the God who is sovereign over them. This leads to a life that is consumed with worries and fears about things beyond our control. But because we have an illusion of control, we wrestle and fight and try to make this life bend to our will—the fruit of which is almost always regret, whether over poor statements made in response to fear, or frustration that life isn't going according to our plans.

If we hope to gain ground in the battle with our tongues, we must entrust everything to God's capable, loving hands. Running the world is an exhausting job and one for which we are not qualified. When we take on that role, it leads to cranky, weary women who wound with their words. We must instead surrender our lives, the lives of those closest to us, and our circumstances, to God. In order to relinquish the idol of control, we need to remind ourselves there is a God and we are not him. We need to remind ourselves the God who created and sustains the universe is quite capable of running it without our help. When we surrender our need for control, we are able to accept failure—whether our own or that of others. We are freed from the insatiable need to have things go our way, and those in our lives feel loved and accepted by us rather than bullied, criticized, or nagged. Surrender doesn't necessarily mean defeat. On the contrary, tremendous freedom, peace, and power comes when we truly surrender control. This in turn leads to women who are happier and more capable of speaking life, instead of death.

POWER

The idol of power is the corrupted desire for success and influence. A woman who is governed by the idol of power has a fierce need to be right, which may lead her to dominate conversations or have the last word. Her relationships may be marked by rivalry, discord, and competition. If she believes others to have an advantage, she may become envious, jealous, and discontent. This then spills out in her speech through being directly quarrelsome and contentious or indirectly grumbling and complaining.

How the idol of power governs a woman's speech will look different for everyone, though there may be some common tendencies:

- It's the woman who always desires to be in the know on things that don't involve her. Knowledge is power and she wants to be its keeper.

- It's the woman who is unwilling to discuss her own weakness, vulnerability, sin, brokenness, and struggles because to do so might threaten her position of power and influence over others. She needs to maintain the perception that she has it all together and may distance herself from others.

- It's the woman who punishes others through criticism or verbal abuse—belittling and demeaning them in front of others.

- It's the woman who dominates conversations and leverages her words over others, manipulating them into doing what she wants.

- It is the woman who feels the need to be at the head of the pack, steering and directing her friend groups. She sees herself as a leader because others tend to follow along with her. What she doesn't realize is that others are often scared to cross her or oppose her ideas for fear of humiliation or retribution; it's just easier to go along with her.

- It's the woman who is extremely competitive and strategically manages to put others down while elevating herself.

- It's the woman who sees people as objects to help her accomplish her own goals or as projects to fix.

- It's the woman who lives by the mantra, "If mama ain't happy, nobody's happy." Her household is her domain to run as she sees fit, and everyone else needs to get with the program or get out of the way. She is the captain of the ship. It's her way or the highway.

Ultimately, the idol of power is rooted in a desire for autonomy—the desire for freedom to run your life how you choose, free from the constraints of another's needs, expectations, or demands. It's a desire to govern your own kingdom, and people are your subjects to do your bidding. It's a desire for influence and prestige. Jesus reminded his disciples the rulers of this world lord their power and flaunt their authority over others, but it should not be so in his kingdom. He said whoever wants to be a leader must be a servant, and whoever wants to be first must be a slave (Mark 6:41–45). Jesus taught that the meek—those who are mild and gentle—will inherit the earth (Matthew 5:5). Meekness is not weakness; nor is it a denial of your strength. On the contrary, meekness is strength and power under restraint. It's a strength that doesn't have to be the first or the best, one that doesn't need to have the last word or dominate conversations. Meekness is a power that has been yielded to the lordship of Christ, power that isn't about selfish gain, but sacrificial service. It's a power that cheerfully and voluntarily steps aside in order to elevate others. Only when we are willing to become weak will Christ's strength be displayed through us (2 Corinthians 2:8–10). Our words will no longer be corrupted expressions governed by a desire for personal power, but a beautiful expression of brotherly love that champions the cause of others.

GRATIFICATION

Blaise Pascal once said that within mankind there is an infinite abyss which can only be filled with an infinite and immutable object, God himself. [6] We are all seeking to fill the god-shaped hole in our lives. We try to fill it with food, people, success, money, and fame. We are starving, longing for satisfaction and fulfillment, but looking in all the wrong places. Nothing truly satisfies. But we often pursue gratification to the detriment of ourselves and others. We become envious, jealous, and bitter. This discontentment can lead to all sorts of corrupted words. Complaining is a big one for me. It's remarkable really; I seem to be able to complain about anything and everything. Every now and then, the Lord opens my ears just long enough to allow me to hear how much negativity and complaining comes out of my mouth.

How the idol of gratification governs a woman's speech will look different for everyone, though there may be some common tendencies:

- It's the wife who is never pleased or satisfied with her life. It could be lack of contentment with material objects, like her house, her car, her clothing. It could be dissatisfaction with her circumstances, like wanting to be a stay-at-home mom when her family needs her to work, or wanting to work when her family needs her to be a stay-at-home mom. Whatever it is, the grass is always greener in someone else's yard. She wants what she doesn't have. Because she frequently expresses her discontent, her husband feels defeated and like he has failed to provide her with a good life.

- It's the single woman who is frustrated because she does not have a spouse. She may gossip and slander married women, criticizing them for not being better wives or for how they should be more grateful for their spouses. Or she may give into words of self-pity, talking with her friends about why other, "more sinful" women are getting engaged or are happily married while she is trying to be faithful and is still single.

- It's the woman who is always complaining and grumbling about life. She feels like she's been dealt a bad hand. She will complain to anyone who will listen, but latches onto those who will affirm and validate her misery.

- It's the woman who envies what others have, often making statements like, "It must be nice to go on a vacation like that" or minimizes other's struggles by saying, "I wish I had your problems."

Ultimately, this idol is fueled by the belief that God has not been kind to you. If someone else has something you don't, you somehow feel slighted. You may suffer from the inaccurate belief that God is supposed to give you the desires of your heart, and any unmet desire feels like he's not living up to his end of the bargain. And so you grumble and complain to others and to God, or you grumble and complain about others and about God. Scripture tells us to do everything without grumbling and complaining (Philippians 2:14). Paul warns that people who long to be rich fall into temptation, and are trapped by foolish and harmful desires that lead to destruction (1 Timothy 6:9). Longing for material goods or children or marriage or career success can lead us to make foolish choices. But worse than our longings are the words we use. Phrases like "If only" or "I wish" or "It must be nice," all of which seem innocent enough, are in actuality an assault on the kindness of God. Instead of grumbling over our lack, we must choose to stand in awe of the gracious blessings God has entrusted to us. We choose to cultivate thankful hearts. We choose to use our words to praise God, thanking him for his many kindnesses. It is God's will for us to rejoice always, pray continually, and give thanks in all things (1 Thessalonians 5:18). This does not mean it will be easy. Some desires are good, legitimate desires. It is good to desire a spouse or a child or financial stability or physical health. These desires aren't bad in and of themselves. But we can identify if they have become idols if we become bitter toward God and others when we do not receive them. In these moments, we must turn again to God—reminding ourselves of his goodness, faithfulness, love, and generosity toward us. We need to gaze upon Christ until he becomes far more magnificent and desirable than the current object of our desire. We become less negative, less envious and, as a result, we grumble and complain less. This not only makes us more pleasant to be around, it gives us an opportunity to lead others in combatting a culture bent on consumption and instant gratification. We may not always feel thankful, but as we practice an attitude of gratitude and make thankfulness part of our daily lives, our speech transforms.

Questions for Reflection

1. Which of these seven idols do you feel is producing the most rotten fruit in your life? (Comfort, Glory, Justice, Approval, Control, Power, Gratification)

2. What does your idolatry expose about your unbelief? What lie are you believing about God that drives you to meet your needs through these inferior substitutes?

SEED OF UNBELIEF

We have just described seven idols that govern our speech, and these are just a few that may have taken up residency in our hearts. Our idolatry is fueled by the unbelief that began in the garden when the serpent planted a seed of suspicion in Eve's heart and mind. Whatever the lie Eve believed—whether it was that God couldn't be trusted or that he was withholding something she needed or deserved—her inaccurate belief about God informed the choice she made. The same is true of us. Before we go much further, let's take a few moments to consider some of the lies we believe that fuel our idolatry:

God is not good.
God does not care.
God does not see me.
God does not love me.
God is not enough.
God is not present and actively engaged in my circumstances.
God has abandoned me.
God is not faithful.
God is not able.
God is not fair.
God is holding out on me.
God cannot be trusted.

It is important to identify the specific lies you believe about God because they are often at the root of corrupted speech. As we nurture these specific lies in our hearts, autonomy sets in, and we act in proud unbelief seeking to meet our needs through the corrupted desires of power, control, approval, justice, gratification, comfort, and glory. These idols produce much fruit in our hearts, but in regards to our speech they produce gossip, slander, a critical spirit, nagging, meddling, and dishonesty—just to name a few!

Now look back at the list above. Can you pick out two or three lies that describe your battle with unbelief? How would you summarize these lies and the actions they lead you to take? Maybe you believe that God isn't good and can't be trusted to protect you, *therefore* you must protect and defend yourself. Or that God doesn't care, *therefore* you must take care of yourself. Taking time to identify what your seed of unbelief is necessary, because this is where transformation begins.

Here is where we have some work to do. We need to figure out what lies we believe, what idol we run to, and what fruit is produced. In order to understand this, we need to examine the soil—the past experiences, present reality, wounds and fears, knowledge and season of life, personal sin struggles and spiritual maturity—that caused the fruit to grow, and then move toward God in faith and repentance. This may feel overwhelming, but it is the good spiritual work of shepherding our souls.

This work takes time and doesn't need to be done alone; we need to invite others into the process. We need to create an atmosphere where the truth can be heard—seeking out people who will tell us the truth and being open to what they have to say. This means regularly talking to others (community/small groups, mentors, friends, spouses) about the fruit we are seeing in our lives and allowing them to ask questions to help us identify the idols and lies. Friends often see clearly where we are blind, so we need to seek out those who won't just say what we want to hear, but who will love us enough to challenge, correct, and encourage us in our speech. When they do so, we must receive it in a spirit of humility, and honestly examine what they say, rather than punishing them or defending ourselves.

SO WHAT CAN YOU DO?

As we have discussed, before words ever form on our tongue, they find roots in the idols of our heart. Here is where we tend to make a grave mistake: *we focus on managing the fruit (our words) rather than addressing the root (our idolatrous heart).* When we manage the fruit, our victories over the tongue are often short-lived. Paul Tripp says these efforts are as futile as nailing fruit on a tree:

> "I am convinced that much of what we do in an attempt to change our communication is nothing more than apple-nailing. It has no energy to understand and confess the war for the heart that lies beneath the war of words. People aren't my problem. Situations are not my problem. Circumstances are not my problem. Locations are not my problem. My problem is in my heart. It's only when you and I stand before our Redeemer and are humbly willing to say, regardless of the flawed people that you live with and the fallen world that is your address, that you are your greatest communication problem, that you are heading in a direction of fundamental biblical change in your world of talk." [7]

What can you do about the problem of your heart? Here is where a graphic may be helpful.

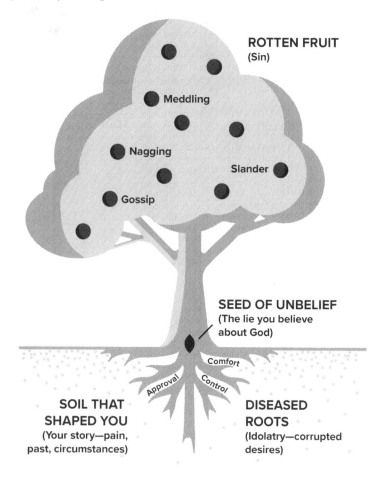

The tree above illustrates everything we've discussed thus far. Many of us spend an inordinate amount of time trying to pluck the bad fruit off of our tree, only to have it grow back over and over again. Or we focus on trying to produce good fruit, only to lapse back into our natural conversational tendencies. The problem is that we are directing our efforts at the wrong thing. *We must trace our rotten fruit back to its diseased root.*

The tree diagram gives us a way to pull all the pieces together and helps get to the root of our speech. Let's take a simple example:

Mary struggles with nagging. She wishes people would just get with it and do what they are supposed to do without being asked or told. Why does she always have to remind people to do the simplest things, like put the dishes away or take the trash out? She has tried to stop nagging people, but she just doesn't seem to be able to for long. She keeps falling back into the same patterns.

The question is why does Mary nag, even when she has a desire to stop? Let's dig a little deeper. When Mary nags people to take the trash out or put things back where they belong, she is seeking order. Her desire for order goes back to the fact that when she was growing up things were chaotic at home. Her mother struggled with hoarding and their house was always a mess. There is nothing wrong with Mary's desire for order; God is a God of order. This desire gets corrupted and becomes an idol when Mary thinks order is ultimate, when she falsely believes it will satisfy and soothe her anxious heart. When people don't meet Mary's need for order she feels out of control and nags until order is re-established in her world. Ultimately, what Mary is doing is orienting her life around the idol of control. This idol is fueled by her unbelief. But what is the lie Mary believes? She believes the illusion that order in her house will settle and satisfy her, helping her feel calm and secure. And she doesn't trust God to provide that for her. But, in reality, God is the only one who can soothe and satisfy the angst in her heart.

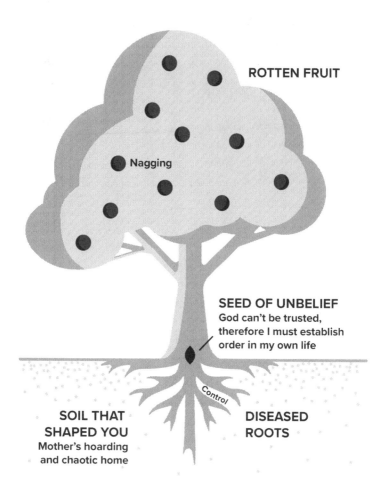

Rotten Fruit: Nagging

Diseased Root: Idol of control

Seed of Unbelief: God can't provide or be trusted, therefore I must establish order

Soil that Shaped Her: Her mother's hoarding and chaotic home

Now, rather than Mary attempting to pluck the rotten fruit of nagging off her tree or securing order in her home through the idol of control, she must turn toward the Lord in faith and repentance. What does

The Root of Our Words

repentance look like for Mary? She must confess the lie she believes about God and and repent of her unbelief. Then, on a daily basis, when she feels anxious and tempted to nag, she must preach the truth of God's trustworthiness and ability to provide for her needs. *This is the work of faith.*

Just like Mary, as we come face-to-face with our sin, we need to confess our unbelief and the lies we've believed. Then we need to move toward Jesus in humble repentance rather than away from him in guilt, shame, and despair. We do this by redirecting all the energy we've spent in unproductive ways—like chasing our idols or plucking bad fruit—and directing it instead toward pressing Jesus deep into our hearts, preaching the truth of Scripture about who God is to our own souls. We need to take every thought captive and make it obedient to Christ. And as we move toward Christ in faith and repentance, he will change our hearts and transform our desires, thereby redeeming our speech and giving us clean lips.

Questions for Reflection

1. In any order you choose, fill in the tree diagram with the following:

- **The Soil that Shaped You:** Write in words that describe your pain, past, and circumstances including your wounds, fears, and current reality.

- **The Seed of Unbelief**: Identify two or three key lies you believe about God. See if you can take these and come up with a phrase that describes your *seed of unbelief.* For example, "I don't believe God is good, therefore I cannot trust him." Or "I don't believe God loves me, therefore I have to prove my worth." This seed of unbelief keeps you from trusting God, fuels your idolatry, and eventually produces rotten fruit.

- **The Diseased Roots**: Label the roots with the main idols you rely on rather than God.

- **The Rotten Fruit:** Label the fruit with words that describe what type of speech comes out of your mouth (for example: gossip, criticism, nagging, belittling, withholding truth, grumbling, lying, exaggerating, rudeness, harshness)

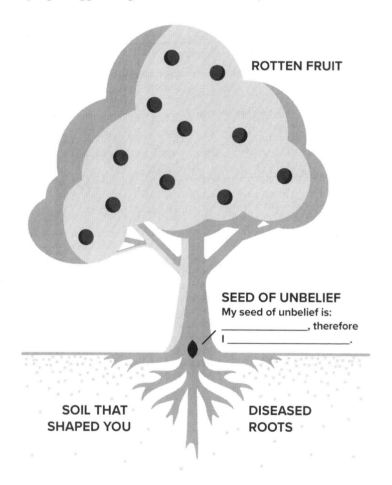

ROTTEN FRUIT

SEED OF UNBELIEF
My seed of unbelief is:
_____, therefore
I _____.

SOIL THAT
SHAPED YOU

DISEASED
ROOTS

2. What are specific truths you need to believe about God to counter your seed of unbelief? Write a phrase that you can memorize and cling to as you fight for faith.

06

GOSSIP

The words of a gossip are like choice morsels; they go down to the inmost parts.

Proverbs 18:8 NIV

When I think about gossip, one story stands out in my mind. It wasn't anything sensational or juicy, so I'm not sure why it made such a mark on me. I was at a restaurant with around twenty or so people at the tail end of a week-long journey. The energy in the room was electric—abuzz with laughter, stories, and shared experiences. At some point during the dinner, the group of women at my end of the table began to discuss someone who wasn't present. It wasn't malicious or mean-spirited, but it also wasn't necessary or kind. I grew more and more uncomfortable as the conversation went along, and not for entirely pure reasons. For one, I was an outsider in the conversation. I hadn't been with them to witness the behaviors of the person they were discussing, so I couldn't relate or join in the dialogue. They had bonded during the experience and now were further solidifying that bond through this conversation. The second reason I was uncomfortable was because what started as one passing comment grew into a fifteen-minute conversation regarding the person's idiosyncrasies and issues. I never said anything or tried to redirect the conversation. Eventually I got up and walked to the other end of the table.

Several years later, I found myself at a different restaurant with a different group of people. The conversation once again shifted to a person who was not at the table. It started with a simple comment or question about the person, and then, just like before, it turned into a long conversation about their current struggles. Similar to my other experience, this wasn't a malicious conversation, but it certainly wasn't a necessary one either. It was a group of people expressing shared concerns and curiosity over what was going on in our friend's life. This time I wasn't the bystander though; I was deep in the middle of it. At some point, I looked across the table and noticed one girl was quiet and looking increasingly uncomfortable. It hit me square between the eyes. We were embroiled in gossip.

God created us to be in fellowship with one another. Much of that fellowship occurs through shared experiences and conversations. We bond with one another, discussing life over a warm cup of coffee or a morning walk. Words help us connect with one another. God entrusted women with a unique capacity to form and nurture relationships; this is part of our *ezer* nature. Even the more introverted among us, including myself, are driven by a desire to have intimate connections with others. It just looks different. Deep down women are driven by a desire to form, solidify, or engage in relationships. This is an essential part of how God created us because it is through these relationships we fulfill God's call on our lives.

Even our brains affirm God's unique design for women. We are hardwired for connection. Neuropsychiatrist Louann Brizendine, who authored the book *The Female Brain*, found women have 11 percent more neurons than men in the brain's centers for language and hearing. Similarly, she discovered that both the hippocampus—the principal hub of emotion and memory formation, as well the brain circuitry for language and observing emotions in others—is also larger in the female brain. [1] These observations led Brizendine to conclude that a woman's verbal agility, her ability to connect deeply in friendships, capacity to read faces and tone of voice to perceive others' emotions and state of mind, and ability to defuse conflict, is accredited to her brain's hardwiring. [2] So if you ever wondered why we have more words than men, now you know!

What I find even more fascinating is Brizendine's discovery that women literally find biological comfort in one another's company! [3] Connecting through talking actually activates the pleasure centers in a woman's brain, releasing the feel good chemical dopamine, as well as the bonding hormone oxytocin. [4] This explains why we long for fellowship and connection with one another—first, because God created us to do so; and second, because our bodies reward us with pleasurable cocktails when we do.

It's clear that God created women with a unique ability to connect with others. But as a result of the fall, every strength has a shadow side. The unique abilities God gave women to establish relational connection and bring strength to others are now the same abilities by which we create division and injure one another. It's the best of who God created us to be working alongside the worst of our fallen nature. It's the old self and the new self simultaneously cohabitating in our flesh (Galatians 5:16–18). When our relational energy, and its attendant gift of gab, is not under the gracious rule of Christ, this God-given power and energy becomes toxic and adversarial to the cause of Christ. Rather than our tongues being tools we use to fulfill our calling as essential counterparts, they become obstacles to overcome, temptations that trip us up along the way.

Gossip and meddling are two common temptations we face as women. We will explore gossip in this chapter and meddling in the next. Each seems to be a regular part of the language of fellowship, interwoven into the fabric of our relationships. The desire to bond with one another is a good, God-honoring desire. We don't always enter into conversations with an intent to gossip or meddle, but it's a slippery slope many of us are careening down before we realize it. If we want to grow in Christ-likeness where our speech is concerned, we must look at the role gossip and meddling plays in our daily lives.

GOSSIP

While gossip is a temptation common to women, it is not an issue limited to women alone. However, I do believe that because God created us with a unique capacity to engage relationally, we are more vulnerable to gossip's allure. Gossip isn't harmless; it's destructive. But it's a sin we often overlook in Christian subculture. We tend to focus far more on so-called bigger sins like pornography, adultery, or premarital sex, somehow viewing gossip as less significant. But Scripture has a far less lenient view toward the sin of gossip—so much so Paul includes gossip in a list of sins alongside murder, greed, and deception (Romans 1:29; 2 Corinthians 12:20). All sin is offensive to God and harmful to ourselves and others; and gossip is no different.

I've had many conversations when it was necessary to discuss another person in order to better help them. That isn't necessarily gossip. But there are plenty of conversations I've had that were pointless gossip. So how do we know what constitutes gossip? The dictionary defines gossip as rumor or report; sharing intimate, personal details about the life of another person. Based on this definition, the information I am sharing may be true or false; it could be fact or conjecture. But that still leaves some questions unanswered. Does that mean I never discuss someone else? Or does it mean I don't say something *about* them that I wouldn't say *to* them?

Concerning gossip, Amy Carmichael once said, "never about, always to." [5] And while there is an element of truth in this statement, it requires more nuance. Perhaps the way Scripture addresses the topic of gossip will bring some needed clarity. The first time we see mention of gossip in Scripture is all the way back in the book of Leviticus. Right in the middle of God's instructions to the Israelites about how to live in right relationship with God and one another, we find God's command,

"Do not spread slanderous gossip among your people" (Leviticus 19:16). The original word for gossip in this verse is *rakil,* which is used five more times in the Old Testament (Proverbs 11:13, 20:19; Jeremiah 6:28, 9:4; Ezekiel 22:9). *Rakil* is often translated in the Bible as a gossip or slanderer; it is someone who is a talebearer or scandalmonger. [6] It's someone who reveals the secrets of others, who betrays confidences and shares personal, even private, information that is not theirs to share. We all know someone who thrives on the latest scandal, or perhaps we've even been the person who runs toward the chaos of another person's life and feeds off the salacious details.

The other word used in the Old Testament for gossip is *nirgan,* which is used four times, all within the book of Proverbs (16:28, 18:8, 26:20, 26:22). A *nirgan,* similar to a *rakil,* is a talebearer or a whisperer. [7] *A whisperer.* Now that paints a vivid picture of gossip! Words shrouded in darkness—shared in hiding and secrecy. I whisper when I don't want anyone to hear what I am saying. There are times when I lower my voice in a public place because the topic of my conversation may be sensitive or personal to me—something I don't want others to hear. And that is entirely appropriate. But there are other kinds of whispering that are far less virtuous.

How do we know if what we are saying in secret is okay? These words from Jesus provide a good litmus test for us:

> Jesus turned first to his disciples and warned them, "Beware of the yeast of the Pharisees—their hypocrisy. The time is coming when everything that is covered up will be revealed, and all that is secret will be made known to all. Whatever you have said in the dark will be heard in the light, and what you have whispered behind closed doors will be shouted from the housetops for all to hear!
>
> Luke 12:1b–3

Whatever you have said in the dark will be heard in the light. What you have whispered behind closed doors will be shouted from the rooftops for all to hear. This passage conjures up all kinds of past conversations I've had! As I read it, I can't help but think about the kinds of things I have whispered that I would be mortified and ashamed of others hearing. In the context of this passage, Jesus is addressing the hypocrisy of the Pharisees—the religious elite who were upright by all external moral standards, but their inner lives were full of wickedness. In essence, Jesus is saying they are not who they portray themselves to be—that who they are in public, doesn't match who they are in private. Living with integrity means who we are in the light of day when others are watching, matches who we are in the dark of night when no one else is around. With this in mind, one way you may be able to diagnose if a conversation is leaning toward gossip is to ask yourself, "Am I saying something about someone else in private that I wouldn't want shouted from the rooftops for all to hear?"

But gossip isn't just about the one talking. The one speaking and the one listening are both engaged. Gossip is a two-way street and destructive for all parties involved. As an ancient text says, the evil tongue slays three, the slanderer, the slandered, and the listener. [8] The author of Proverbs tells us wrongdoers eagerly listen to gossip (17:4). We may not even repeat the gossip, but if we find ourselves leaning in to hear the details and somehow feeling satisfied by our newfound knowledge, then we are likely engaging in the act of gossip. Twice the writer of Proverbs says, "The words of a gossip are like choice morsels; they go down to the inmost parts" (18:8, 26:22). The idea behind this statement is that we gobble them up. We have an appetite for gossip.

Many times, we gossip out of a deep desire to belong. Sometimes we gossip to make ourselves feel better by pointing out another's flaws or failures. We might use it to solidify connection with others in situations where we feel socially awkward. Or we gossip as a way of gaining status by being the reporter, the one in the know. And sometimes we

LIVING WITH INTEGRITY

MEANS WHO WE ARE IN THE

LIGHT OF DAY WHEN OTHERS

ARE WATCHING, MATCHES WHO

WE ARE IN THE DARK OF NIGHT

WHEN NO ONE ELSE IS AROUND.

even cloak it in a veil of spirituality through a prayer request or by presenting it as concern for a friend.

Slander and gossip are bedfellows, with one slight distinction. Slander is publicly sharing false information with willful intent to harm a person's reputation. Gossip, on the other hand, is usually done in secret and may or may not be done with ill-will, and it may or may not be true. Gossip is often full of rumor, conjecture, or hearsay. So for the purpose of this study, we will define gossip as *sharing information about someone, true or not, that does not benefit them or the listener.*

With this definition in view, gossip could include talking about someone we know and love and revealing their personal information to a third party. We may not necessarily have ill-intent, but the information we are sharing doesn't benefit our friend or the person we are talking to. For example, a friend of mine recently shared a story with me about her own temptation toward gossip. Her friend Tim approached her and asked her what was going on with their mutual friend Kristin. Tim was concerned because Kristin had canceled several meetings with him and he was worried about her. My friend shared with Tim that Kristin was having some health issues and both of them expressed how sad they were about Kristin's current circumstances. This is not necessarily gossip. But my friend noticed she was on a slippery slope toward gossip when she wanted to go beyond that and share more of the details of Kristin's life with him—details he didn't really need to know. My friend loves Kristin and had no malice in wanting to share the details, but she realized it wasn't HER story to tell without permission.

This can be challenging because sometimes you feel like you aren't being truthful. Recently, I became aware of a friend of mine who was having trouble in her marriage. Most of the information I had about her situation had come through others. Even though I had been in recent contact with her, she had not chosen to share any of her story with me personally. So when another friend approached me and asked me about her, I shared only what my friend had directly told me, information which I knew she would be okay with me repeating. When my other friend pressed me further and told me she had heard about the marital troubles, my response was "I'm really not sure. She hasn't shared any of that with me." Even if she had, it still wouldn't have been my story to tell. I would have been stealing something deeply personal from her. But in that moment, I knew I had other true information that I was not disclosing, and I somehow felt icky about hiding it from our other friend.

There is also a darker side to gossip—one that is more self-serving. We could be gratifying desires for justice or attempting to strengthen our own fragile egos by sharing information about another person. Ray Ortlund describes gossip in this way:

> Gossip spreads what can include accurate information to diminish another person . . . Gossip is our dark moral fervor eagerly seeking gratification. Gossip makes us feel important and needed as we declare our judgments. It makes us feel included to know the inside scoop. It makes us feel powerful to cut someone else down to size, especially someone we are jealous of. It makes us feel righteous, even responsible to pronounce someone else guilty. Gossip can feel good in multiple ways. But it is of the flesh, not of the Spirit. [9]

Whether our intent is seemingly innocent or more self-serving, Proverbs is clear about the relational implications of gossip:

- A troublemaker plants seeds of strife; gossip separates the best of friends (16:28).

- A gossip betrays a confidence; so avoid anyone who talks too much (20:19 NIV).

- When arguing with your neighbor, don't betray another person's secret. Others may accuse you of gossip, and you will never regain your good reputation (25:9–10).

- As surely as a north wind brings rain, so a gossiping tongue causes anger (25:23).

- Fire goes out without wood, and quarrels disappear when gossip stops (26:20).

According to Scripture gossip is betrayal (11:13; 20:19); separates friends (16:28); incites anger (25:23); fuels quarrels (26:20); and ruins your own reputation and credibility (25:10). Ultimately, gossip is destructive, not constructive. It is hurtful, not helpful. Rather than strengthening our relationships with others, it weakens or even destroys them altogether.

Gossip not only harms the individual you are talking about, it also harms the person you are talking to by placing the burden of knowledge on them. Words are sticky; once you know something about someone, you can't unknow it. Knowledge carries with it the burden of responsibility—you are responsible for what you know and also for what you do with what you know. This reminds me of a conversation I once had when someone assumed I had knowledge of a situation involving a third party that I didn't. Even though the situation had occurred years before, the image I had of the third party shifted in my mind ever so slightly. I couldn't erase it or forget it. On top of that, I still have to carry it; I have to be responsible for how I steward that knowledge. Perhaps that is what led the author of Ecclesiastes to cry out, "The greater my wisdom, the greater my grief. To increase knowledge, only increases sorrow" (Ecclesiastes 1:18).

Imagine a person's reputation is like a puzzle. Pieces of the puzzle are made up by that person's actions, how they live their lives, and the words they use as they interact with others. But the words you speak *about* them *to* others are also pieces of that puzzle. Over time an image of the person begins to form and your words make up a part of the image. In that way, gossip is not a minor, insignificant issue. It can be a verbal assault on another person's character and reputation. It doesn't matter, in this instance, if the information you are sharing is true or false. Either way, the information you shared shapes, even mars, that person's image in the eyes of another. It's like splattering paint on the *Mona Lisa*—they might still be able to see her, but they have to look past the splatter.

There are times when we need to discuss someone with others. Parents need to be able to discuss their children in order to address issues. A boss may need to discuss an employee's poor performance with the human resources department in order to establish a performance plan. A small group leader may need to discuss someone in their group with a pastor in order to seek guidance on how to lead them through a certain situation. A husband or wife may need to discuss their spouse with a trusted mentor in order to gain wisdom and a biblical perspective. And a friend may need to seek guidance from an outside party on how to address conflict in a relationship. This is part of life.

But notice in all of these scenarios, the goal is a collaborative effort to pursue wisdom, understanding, and direction where the other person is concerned. The undercurrent in these situations is about seeking that person's highest good and strengthening or restoring relationships. The issue isn't just not talking about someone else; the issue is also *how* we talk about them and *what* we say when they're not around. How would I feel if the other person were to hear me speak about them the way that I am? Are the words I use about them or their situation honoring or are they hurtful and demeaning? Will what I share and how I share it be a blessing to the person I am talking about?

We might be able to identify gossip by the words that precede it. Words like, "Don't tell anyone this . . . " or "You didn't hear this from me . . . " or "Have you heard about . . ." or "Keep this between us." Whenever these phrases are uttered, gossip almost certainly follows.

It is also an issue of concern versus responsibility. You may have legitimate cause for concern, but you have no ability to impact the situation. Therefore, a faithful response is to entrust the person and the situation to God and not discuss it with others. In the case of my friend's troubled marriage, while I was concerned for her, I was not responsible

WORDS ARE STICKY;

ONCE YOU KNOW SOMETHING

ABOUT SOMEONE, YOU CAN'T

UNKNOW IT. KNOWLEDGE

CARRIES WITH IT THE BURDEN

OF RESPONSIBILITY—YOU ARE

RESPONSIBLE FOR WHAT YOU

KNOW AND ALSO FOR WHAT YOU

DO WITH WHAT YOU KNOW.

for her. She had not invited me or our other friend into her life in that way. So for us to talk about it would have been gossip.

As we stated earlier, gossip may be true or it may be false. Slander, on the other hand, is to make a false, defamatory statement about someone. It is lying or misrepresenting someone publicly in such a way that damages character and ruins their reputation in the eyes of others. The ninth commandment says, "You must not testify falsely against your neighbor." While this commandment was primarily concerned about bearing false witness against another person in a court of law, it can be expanded to "include any situation in which untrue words are used to harm another individual." [10]

The Westminster Larger Catechism brings clarity on the ninth commandment and the importance of truthfulness by listing some of the sins that could be included:

- Prejudicing the truth and the good name of our neighbors
- Speaking the truth unseasonably or maliciously to a wrong end or perverting it to a wrong meaning
- Speaking untruth
- Lying, slandering, backbiting, detracting, talebearing, whispering, scoffing, reviling, rash, harsh, and partial censoring
- Misconstructing intentions, words, and actions
- Raising false rumors, receiving and countenancing evil reports
- Rejoicing in others' disgrace and infamy

The catechism goes beyond just declaring what we should not do where the ninth commandment is concerned; it provides a vision for how we can bless others with our speech as well. Some of these duties toward our neighbor include:

- Preserving and promoting of truth between man and man, and the good name of our neighbor
- A charitable esteem of our neighbors
- Loving, desiring, and rejoicing in their good name
- Sorrowing for and covering of infirmities
- Freely acknowledging gifts and graces and defending innocence
- A ready receiving of a good report and an unwillingness to admit of an evil report concerning them
- Discouraging talebearers, flatterers, and slanderers [11]

Whether the issue is gossip or slander, whether true or false, the Bible intends for our speech toward our neighbor to be truthful and to bless rather than curse. We have a responsibility to promote and defend the good name of our neighbors, and to not speak of them in a way that would sway another's opinion or view of them.

How do we navigate the slippery slope of gossip? Here are a few practical things we can do:

- Ask for permission to share the contents of your conversation.
- Set expectations in shepherding relationships that the contents of a conversation may at some point need to be discussed with another.
- Change the subject when someone starts to gossip.
- When someone is gossiping or slandering another, step in and offer a different perspective about the situation.

I've used the last two on many occasions and have found they work well. When you feel like a conversation is getting out of hand, ask the person who's gossiping about their day or their plans for the weekend or their kids. It might feel like an abrupt shift in the conversation, but that's okay. People tend to move right into the next part of the conversation without missing a beat. I've also found the last suggestion helpful. If the person gossiping is talking about how a coworker has been slacking off lately, say something like, "Maybe she's having a bad week" or "That's not like her. I hope she's okay. I'll be praying for her." When people see you aren't going to jump on the bandwagon, the conversation will die a natural death. Whatever you do, pause and choose your first response with precision and care to ensure that you don't fan the flames.

Gossip also raises the question about venting. What do you do when you are upset and need to discuss a situation involving another person? How can you handle this faithfully, in a way that honors the other person involved? Here are some things to consider:

- Consider the person you are venting to. Are they spiritually mature? Can they faithfully handle the information you are sharing with them? Will they tell you the truth and not just take your side?

- Consider the reason you want to vent. Are you seeking wisdom and direction for how to handle the situation? Do you need to process through your emotions in order to see the situation more clearly? Or are you just seeking someone to commiserate with and who will affirm your rightness and desire for justice and retribution?

- Are there other options you could consider that would not involve going to another person? If you are a verbal processor, journaling is an excellent way to vent, process through emotions, and seek wisdom and clarity on what next steps to take.

- When you really just need to blow off some steam, leave names and details out that could identify the person you are discussing in order to preserve their honor and dignity.

- You may need to go exercise or do something physical to burn off some energy, which will enable you to think more clearly and see the situation from a fresh perspective.

Finally, let's not underestimate God's ability to handle the full range of our emotions and to lead us with all wisdom. Through his Spirit, he can provide clarity to help us see the situation rightly, guiding us in how to respond in a way that honors all involved.

As we saw in the first chapter, we were created to bring strength and life to the relationships around us. Communication is one of the key ways in which we do this. But gossip and slander destroy rather than nurture relationships and, therefore, hinder us from living out our *ezer* calling.

Questions for Reflection

1. In what situations are you most tempted to gossip? Why do you think that is?

2. What idol do you think is at the root of your need to gossip? What lie are you believing that is causing you to gossip?

3. Have you ever been wounded by gossip or slander? How did that impact you?

4. What is a realistic strategy you could use to redirect a conversation?

5. Is the current way in which you vent a healthy way to process what you are thinking and feeling? What changes do you need to make?

07

MEDDLING

[W]e hear that some of you are living idle lives, refusing to work and meddling in other people's business. We command such people and urge them in the name of the Lord Jesus Christ to settle down and work to earn their own living.

2 Thessalonians 3:11

As we explored in the previous chapter, gossip and meddling are common temptations for women. *Meddling is interfering or inserting yourself in someone's life without an invitation, or involving yourself in something that you are not responsible for with the goal of achieving a certain outcome.* Meddling can be overt or covert; direct and indirect. Either way, meddling sabotages relationships and causes division. Proverbs 26:17 says, "Interfering in someone else's argument is as foolish as yanking a dog's ears." Anyone who has ever offered unsolicited advice or an unsolicited opinion understands the humor embedded in this verse. There are at least a handful of times I am reminded of offering my unsolicited opinion to someone only to have them snap at me. Just like you shouldn't be offended or act surprised when a dog bites you for pulling his ears, you shouldn't be surprised when someone bites you for interfering in their affairs without an invitation.

This can get sticky because often we want to help. I remember calling a friend one time who was expressing some things on social media that seemed to be inviting chaos and disruption into her life. We have a close relationship, so I assumed she would be open to what I had to say. When I called and expressed my concern she became defensive and lashed out with harsh words. A similar thing happened one day when she called me to vent about something her husband did. As I began to offer a different perspective, she again launched a verbal assault that left me gun shy and licking my wounds. Because of our close relationship, one would naturally assume I'd earned a hearing in her life. But what I learned is that sometimes, instead of inserting ourselves, we have to be invited in.

This can also be said of mothers and their adult children. I've heard countless women share frustration over the constant meddling of their mothers-in-law, as well as husbands who are trying to navigate the treacherous terrain of their wives' overly involved mothers. The temptation as a mom is huge. We were there when they were unable to care for themselves, meeting their needs and helping solve their problems. But as they age and take on an identity and life of their own, they no longer need or want us in the same way they used to. If we don't make the adjustment in how we relate to our adult children, especially our married adult children, what we consider mothering may very well be meddling.

A wise woman once told me she is careful not to offer unsolicited advice or insights to her adult children. If they call her and share a particularly challenging part of their lives, she is there to listen. But before she says anything to them she asks for an invitation, saying something along the lines of, "I am so sorry you are dealing with that. I can tell you are frustrated (sad, angry, scared). How can I help you? Would you like my perspective or help thinking through it?" By doing this, she gives them permission to choose to invite her to speak into their lives or to decline. This requires great restraint on a mother's part, because by nature she wants to help. But it also requires a tremendous amount of trust in God because it's hard to watch your children struggle and try to make their way through life. If we are honest with ourselves though, our efforts at helping are often as much about alleviating our own anxieties regarding our children as they are about trying to advise them. It is a whole lot harder to entrust them to God than it is to trust our own abilities to swoop in to save the day.

Asking for an invitation to speak is one way to avoid meddling. This can be used with friends, family, and colleagues. There are some situations though where the invitation is implied, such as in accountability relationships or small groups. When someone chooses to join a small group, they are placing themselves in the care of the community and the group leaders. Though it's not always the case, most of the time their willing participation indicates they're open to others speaking into their lives.

Because we are often deceived by what we perceive as good intentions and desires to help, we might benefit by some specific ways meddling manifests in the lives of women:

- Social media voyeurism: peering into the lives of those whom you have little to no face-to-face contact with

- Giving unsolicited advice to your adult children on parenting, marriage, finances, and other issues

- Attempting to control or manipulate an outcome in a situation you don't belong in and are not responsible for

- Covertly operating behind the scenes to achieve a desired outcome, whether a date for your daughter, promotion for your husband, or trying to find the perfect roommate for your son at college

- Operating behind the scenes like a puppet master to resolve conflict between two adults—whether children, coworkers, neighbors, or friends, rather than giving them room to resolve things on their own

WHEN YOU OFFER

TO HELP AND THE OTHER

PERSON DECLINES AND

YOU HELP ANYWAY, THAT IS

NOT HELPING, THAT IS

MEDDLING.

- Becoming hurt or offended when your unsolicited information, instruction, or advice isn't appreciated

- Nudging your grown daughter disapprovingly over her menu choice, while her husband and children look on, and then wondering why she and her family don't want to spend time with you.

- Thriving on being needed and being in the center of things, and seeking out ways to be included.

- Dropping hints, like "Are you sure you want to do that?" or "You're not going to (fill in the blank), are you?" with the desire to steer in a favored direction.

Often the more intimate the relationship, the more you may be tempted to meddle in an effort to assuage your own discomfort, prevent suffering, or make yourself indispensable in the lives of others. Many times this comes from an elevated sense of self and a desire to be indispensable. In reality, meddling is a corrupt form of nurture. The difference between help and meddling is permission. *When you offer to help and the other person declines and you help anyway, that is not helping, that is meddling.*

Questions for Reflection

1. In what relationships and circumstances are you tempted to meddle? What does that look like in your own life? Do your adult children avoid you? Are your teenage children or their friends frustrated with your overreach into their lives? What other relationships are damaged because of your meddling?

2. What idol do you think is at the root of your meddling?

3. What lie are you believing that is causing you to meddle?

CONCERN VS. RESPONSIBILITY

As we have seen already, meddling is a fruit driven by our idols of approval, control, power and so forth. However, an additional reason we struggle with meddling is that we aren't clear on what we are responsible for and what is a concern. This leads us to expend our excess energy on the wrong things rather than focusing our energies on what we alone are responsible for. A *concern is something which you are legitimately concerned about but have no ability to impact.* Because of this, a concern must be entrusted to God. However, a *responsibility is something you alone can do and for which God will hold you accountable.* [1] In the diagram below, the responsibility circle is much smaller than the concern circle, which indicates there are a few things for which you alone are responsible, while many others things in life are concerns. When we do not entrust our concerns to God, we are tempted to meddle and involve ourselves in situations we *aren't* responsible for and neglect the things we *are* on the hook for.

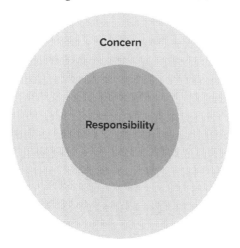

Questions for Reflection

Use the Concern vs. Responsibility chart on the previous page to take inventory of your current season of life.

- In the responsibility circle write in everything you are actively responsible for right now.

- In the concern circle write in everything that is a legitimate concern right now, but you have no ability to impact.

Use the questions below to help determine whether or not to adjust anything in either circle. As we enter into new seasons of life, we need to constantly make adjustments to our circles of responsibility and concern. Make the needed changes in the empty diagram below these questions.

1. Is there anything in the responsibility circle that is actually not your responsibility? Should it be moved to the concern circle?

2. Are their areas of your life that you *are* responsible for that are suffering because you are spending energy on concerns and other frivolous things?

3. Is there anything in the concern circle that is *actually* a responsibility you are ignoring? If so, move it to the responsibility circle.

4. As you look at your circles, which one is consuming most of your energy? If the answer is your concerns, then adjustments need to be made. We each have a limited amount of energy and it needs to be spent on our responsibilities. Concerns we must entrust to God.

5. Do you have too much responsibility or not enough? If too much, do you have concerns that are masquerading as responsibilities that need to be shifted to the other circle? If not enough, are you avoiding responsibilities, and if so why? What can you do to add more responsibility into your life?

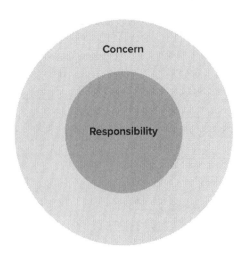

PAUL'S WARNINGS ABOUT IDLENESS

The New Testament deals with the subject of meddling in three different passages. The first passage occurs in 1 Peter 4:14-15, "If you are insulted because you bear the name of Christ, you will be blessed, for the glorious Spirit of God rests upon you. If you suffer, however, it must not be for murder, stealing, making trouble, or prying into other people's affairs." Peter expects Christians to suffer. And there is no shame in suffering because we are followers of Jesus. In fact, this kind of suffering isn't pointless or fruitless; it brings much glory to God and is worthy of our aspirations. But he warns not to bring suffering on ourselves through our own sinful actions—like murder, stealing, or meddling. In this way, the suffering we experience is justified and fruitless. It's funny to me, in an unnerving way, that Peter included meddling alongside murder and stealing. How many of us think of ourselves as good Christians because we've never committed murder or stolen from anyone, and yet few of us can claim we've never meddled.

The apostle Paul also tackled a form of meddling in both 2 Thessalonians and 1 Timothy. He referred to this as being a busybody. Being a busybody is similar to meddling and gossip in that a busybody is overly interested in the affairs of other people. It's fixating on what others are doing instead of focusing on what you are supposed to be doing. [2] As we look at how Paul addresses the issue of being a busybody in these two passages, a common root issue comes to light.

> [W]e hear that some of you are living idle lives, refusing to work and meddling in other people's business. We command such people and urge them in the name of the Lord Jesus Christ to settle down and work to earn their own living.
>
> 2 Thessalonians 3:11

In this passage, Paul admonished believers living idle lives because they were being disruptive and meddling in others' affairs. Instead of being busy workers, they were being busybodies. He challenged them to stop busying themselves in the affairs of others and to work quietly and earn their own living. By doing so, they wouldn't have time to be concerned with the affairs of others.

A similar idea emerges in Paul's letter to Timothy, when he instructs Timothy on how to best care for culturally vulnerable widows:

> A widow who is put on the list for support must be a woman who is at least sixty years old and was faithful to her husband. She must be well respected by everyone because of the good she has done. Has she brought up her children well? Has she been kind to strangers and served other believers humbly? Has she helped those who are in trouble? Has she always been ready to do good?

The younger widows should not be on the list, because their physical desires will overpower their devotion to Christ and they will want to remarry. Then they would be guilty of breaking their previous pledge. And if they are on the list, they will learn to be lazy and will spend their time gossiping from house to house, meddling in other people's business and talking about things they shouldn't. So I advise these younger widows to marry again, have children, and take care of their own homes. Then the enemy will not be able to say anything against them. For I am afraid that some of them have already gone astray and now follow Satan.

1 Timothy 5:9-15

In both passages, Paul connects idleness with gossiping and being busybodies. We might consider idleness to be the same as laziness, but while it may include laziness, idleness is more than that. When a car engine idles, it is running; it just isn't going anywhere. It's the same with an idle person. They're burning energy, but it's frivolous, superficial, pointless; it isn't fruitful or profiting anyone. Eventually it can even become destructive, which is exactly what Paul was worried about.

Paul gave Timothy explicit instructions not to place the young widows on the benevolence list. Paul feared that if the young widows were put on the list they would grow restless of being single and desire to remarry, in which case their natural sexual impulses might overcome their dedication to Christ and lead them to break their commitment. [3] Paul's second concern was they would learn to be idle and spend their time going from house to house gossiping and being busybodies. It's clear Paul wasn't concerned about them expending energy; his concern was *how* they would expend it. Paul wanted to keep them from becoming disruptive to the church. For that reason, Paul encouraged Timothy to have the young widows marry—to live their own lives and concern themselves with their own work—which would keep them from traveling from house to house meddling and gossiping. According to Paul, idleness leads to toxic energy.

ENERGY AND RESPONSIBILITY

This instruction might sound strange in our culture, but it has important present-day implications. It appears Paul was drawing a connection between work and the corruption of our relational capacities through gossip and meddling. But before diving into the practical application, let me first clarify that Paul's instruction regarding younger widows does not mean every woman is supposed to get married and have children and stay at home. Nor does it mean that every woman is supposed to have a job. The point is we all need to be responsible; we need to invest our energy in fruitful and productive ways. Everyone— man, woman, and child—needs to work. Work is good; God works. He worked to create the universe and he continues to work in sustaining it. Work is not a career or a job; it is embracing responsibility. *Work is the intentional employment of your energy and gifts to strengthen those entrusted to you, and to remake the world around you so that God's glory and goodness are increasingly evident.*

God created you with unique gifts and talents. He has given you wisdom and understanding through the specific experiences you've had in life—whether good or bad ones. You have learned wisdom from suffering, either at the hands of another or through your own sinful choices. You also have good gifts God has given, and joys he has allowed you to experience. All of this makes up who you are. And your work, as a woman, is to steward it all by coming alongside others—using it to fill in the gaps and meet the needs of the vulnerable.

It seems this was in view as Paul gave Timothy instruction on how to determine which widows to support:

> A widow who is put on the list for support must be a woman who is at least sixty years old and was faithful to her husband.

> She must be well respected by everyone because of the good she has done. Has she brought up her children well? Has she been kind to strangers and served other believers humbly? Has she helped those who are in trouble? Has she always been ready to do good?

1 Timothy 5:9-10

Paul's qualifications for being placed on the list for support is that these women were known for their good *work*. These women had embraced what they were directly responsible for—their own marriage and children; but they also took on personal responsibility to be hospitable to strangers, serve other believers and impart relief to those who were troubled. They labored in such a way that others benefitted from their expended energy. They gave aid from their own resources and directed their energy toward what was fruitful and profitable for others, rather than busying themselves with trivial, unimportant things that benefitted no one.

This is the kind of woman qualified to be placed on the support list for widows—one who has given her life working for the good of those around her. A woman who has poured herself out—who has spent herself on behalf of others—doesn't have excess energy stored up. *The problem occurs when we have excess energy that gets mismanaged or misdirected—that is when our energy becomes toxic.* We must do more than harness or restrain that energy; we must redirect in more appropriate ways that are fruitful and productive for the cause of Christ.

Below are three bar graphs that illustrate the relationship between energy and responsibility:

Mythical Balance: This is where energy and responsibility are balanced. The mistake we make is assuming balance is the goal. We reject sacrifice, suffering, and responsibility to pursue ease, comfort and happiness—the fruit of which is self-reliance.

Corrupted Energy: This is where our energy level exceeds our responsibility. The mistake we make here is rejecting responsibility

WORK IS THE INTENTIONAL

EMPLOYMENT OF YOUR ENERGY

AND GIFTS TO STRENGTHEN

THOSE ENTRUSTED TO YOU,

AND TO REMAKE THE WORLD

AROUND YOU SO THAT GOD'S

GLORY AND GOODNESS ARE

INCREASINGLY EVIDENT.

and bleeding off energy in toxic, self-absorbed ways—the fruit of which is arrogance, self-righteousness, judgmentalness, laziness, and spiritual atrophy.

Faithful Stewardship: This is where our responsibilities exceed our energy and capabilities. A gap is created that we fill with faith and dependence on God and others. Faithful stewardship produces humility, strength, wisdom, and spiritual maturity.

CORRUPTED ENERGY	THE MYTHICAL BALANCE	FAITHFUL STEWARDSHIP
ENERGY / DEFICIT / RESPONSIBILITY	ENERGY / RESPONSIBILITY	FAITH / ENERGY / RESPONSIBILITY

The Creator of the universe entrusted you with the capacity to make the world better by owning the cause of the weak and vulnerable around you. You are wired for it; this is what God created you to do—to find people who have a deficit, who are underserved, and to bring strength to bear in a way that changes their lives for the better. It is when our energy exceeds responsibility that we create trouble for ourselves and others. This is depicted in the *Corrupted Energy* bar graph. When a gap is created by having too much energy and not enough real responsibility, this leads to idleness, discontentment, and restlessness—exactly what the apostle Paul was concerned about. This is when we find ourselves getting overly involved in the lives of others; focused on unhealthy obsessions that disrupt family, life, work, and other relationships; investing in foolish, time-consuming activities that don't produce fruit.

Because this energy must be expelled, we start looking for ways to burn it off. Sometimes we go shopping and spend money we shouldn't. Other times we criticize someone else's parenting skills. Perhaps we burn hours bingeing on movies or television shows. Or we stand on the sidelines, judging and criticizing someone else's work that has nothing to do with us. But perhaps one of the clearest ways in today's culture is we insert ourselves into the lives of others via social media. Rather than roaming from house to house, gossiping and meddling, we now wander from feed to feed. We keep ourselves in the know, ever-scrolling for fear of missing out on something good. This is a problem because we are concerning ourselves with what we aren't directly responsible for. *Rather than burning energy on something productive and helpful, we burn it on something trivial at best and disruptive at worst.*

As followers of Jesus, we should work harder than we feel we have energy for concerning things for which we are clearly responsible. This is depicted in the *Faithful Stewardship* bar graph. It's not just being busy though. We can be busy with a thousand little things that require little to no thought or effort. Being responsible for something, as opposed to just being busy, means we are accountable. We are clearly carrying the load—physically, mentally, emotionally, and spiritually. This leaves little mental or emotional energy to engage in things that have nothing to do with us. It also pushes us beyond what we feel can be accomplished on our own. That gap—between energy and responsibility—is faith. When what we are responsible for exceeds the amount of energy we have, it pushes us beyond self-sufficiency to faith and dependence on God and others.

We must resist the temptation to compare our responsibility load or energy level to that of another woman. Every woman's capacity is different. Some women have a higher capacity than others. Similarly, everyone's life circumstances are different. It's important to recognize many factors contribute to energy level: age, physical ailments, season of life, and current circumstances. It reminds me of the widow who offered up her two small coins, while many around her put in large amounts. Jesus commended her faithfulness because she gave all of what she had while others gave a small amount out of their surplus

(Mark 12:41–43). *The standard of measurement is not how much energy you have, but the faithful stewardship of what you do have.*

There are times, however, when our lives are in crisis mode through no fault of our own. We have not deliberately stepped outside of the boundaries of faith—overreaching and overfunctioning by dragging concerns into the realm of responsibility—but life's circumstances have overwhelmed us with the burden of responsibility. It may be having three children still in diapers, or a health crisis with a family member who needs care and attention. In these seasons, we need to seek guidance from biblical community. They can help us determine what activities we need to let go in order to direct our time, energy, and effort toward the things we are responsible for in the season of crisis.

Balance isn't the goal. *The goal is to live in the gap of faith—stretched just beyond what we believe we are capable of and wholly dependent on God to do what we cannot do on our own.* This humbles us, leading us to treat one another with compassion. We know what it's like to carry heavy loads, so we are more patient and kind to one another. We are less likely to step on one another's toes, inserting ourselves in things that have nothing to do with us. We are less likely to criticize, judge, meddle, and gossip.

Being a disciple of Jesus involves suffering, discipline, death, and making disciples. We are called to bear one another's burdens. This is hard work. In his letter to the Philippians, Paul said he was being poured out as a drink offering on the altar of their faith (2:17), and this is what we are called to do for others as a follower of Jesus Christ—pour ourselves out on their behalf. Our lives should be impoverished in such a way that other people are the benefactors. This is the work we've been called to do.

SO HOW DO WE DO THIS?

The Scripture calls us to be faithful stewards of what God has entrusted to us. This requires faith and obedience. If we aren't biblically literate, we will be blown about by whatever sounds good and appeals to our sinful desires. To have the necessary wisdom to direct our time and energy faithfully, we must become biblically literate—regularly reading Scripture to learn who God is, what he values, what he desires from us.

Second, let's heed Paul's exhortation to the Galatians, "Pay careful attention to your own work, for then you will get the satisfaction of a job well done, and you won't need to compare yourself to anyone else. For we are each responsible for our own conduct" (Galatians 6:4-5). What is your work? What are you responsible for? Who is depending on you? How are you spending your time? When we spend our energy on our own work, we have no time or energy left to compare or criticize, gossip or meddle.

So what might this look like in different seasons of life?

If you are a young woman who is single and still living at home, you are living in the shade others have created for you. This can lead to underreaching, underfunctioning, and arrogance if you aren't careful. I know; I was a teenage girl too. It's tempting to stand in judgment of your parents, criticizing and slandering them to your peers. Bearing the burden of responsibility and the suffering that comes from work will humble you. Because this is often a season where you have tons of freedom and little responsibility, you have tons of energy to burn. This can leave you vulnerable to the temptations of sexual immorality, gossip, and spending your life frivolously on social media. In this season, it is important to channel excess energy in ways that honor and glorify Christ. Intentionally seek responsibility—whether getting a part-time job, serving on student council, tutoring at-risk youth, or investing in women younger than you. Be responsible for something and spend your energy in ways that profit the kingdom of God and the world around you.

As a single woman who is in the working world, it's common to spend inordinate amounts of time thinking about yourself and structuring your life so you are at the center. As a woman who didn't get married until I was thirty-five, I spent much of my time and energy on myself. You can get caught up in planning for your future and investing in your own goals, dreams, and desires. The temptation is to build a perfect life for yourself—spending large amounts of time, energy, and money on things that only benefit you. But the time, energy, and talents you have are not your own. They don't belong to you, and they aren't meant to be spent on just you. This is a time to think about the needs around you and how you can invest in others and pour yourself out.

For married women, you have a unique opportunity to bring strength in the context of your marriage relationship and learn how to help those under your influence flourish. As a wife, it's easy to think your husband doesn't need you. That misconception can lead you to abdicate your responsibility to learn how you can invest in your husband. Rather than directing your energy toward strengthening him and investing in your marriage, you spend hours engaged in fruitless endeavors like documenting your lives on social media or building a dream life on your Pinterest board. There isn't anything wrong with social media. The problem is when you invest more time and energy into figuring out the perfect paint color for your den or trying to become an influencer on social media than you spend learning how to encourage and speak life into your spouse.

If you are married with children or a single mom, I want to encourage you. This is a time when you don't feel you have extra energy or margin. It might cause you to feel guilty or inadequate. You may compare yourself to other moms who seem to be able to do it all when you are struggling to remember to feed your child before rushing them out the door to school. The danger in this season is to despair and resent not having freedom and margin in your life. Stay focused on what God has called you to. You are doing good work—work that has generational implications.

If your children are older, it is important to start intentionally thinking about this new season of your life. You will find yourself with excess energy—energy that used to be spent directing them, but is no longer required because they are now more self-directed. This is often a difficult transition for women to make, especially those who have had the opportunity to stay at home with their children. Now that your children are older, how can you begin to strategically deploy that energy in other areas? If the energy is not redeployed in healthy and productive ways, it can lead to overreaching and overfunctioning—hovering, nagging, and being overly involved in your children's lives. You have specific gifts the Lord has entrusted to you that are important and necessary to his kingdom. Look for those that are vulnerable and see how you can invest your time, energy, and gifts to make their lives better.

And if your children are grown and no longer at home, this is the time to do the difficult but good work, to figure out what you are going to do in the second half of your life. Being intentional takes effort, work, and time. You are far more valuable to the world and to the body of Christ now than you were twenty years ago. As an empty nester, I see the temptation to move into a life of ease and comfort. I have margin to do things now that I haven't had for years. It would be easy, once again, to structure a life that is all about me. But there is work to do. Jesus said the harvest is ready, but the workers are few. The body of Christ needs you; it needs the kind of faith and wisdom and experience that can only be forged over decades. Idleness is not an option.

Regardless of our season of life, this requires wisdom and direction from outside ourselves. We need to seek God in prayer, giving him an opportunity to speak into our lives and redirect our paths. We also need to seek wise counsel and surround ourselves with other believers attempting to do the same thing. And finally, we need to begin moving; we need to start using the time and gifts God has entrusted to us. Over time, he will provide clarity on your gifts, your energy level and how you can sustain it, and whether or not you are going beyond the boundaries of faith in what you are doing.

The point is to learn how to be faithful stewards of the time, energy, and gifts the Lord has entrusted to us in whatever season of life we are in, so we don't become disruptive to our families, our churches, and our communities by wasting time gossiping and meddling. By being faithful, our families, churches, and communities will flourish—in part because we have been a willing vessel the Lord is working through.

Questions for Reflection

1. Do any of the seasonal descriptions give insight into your own season of life? What changes do you need to make to create an energy and responsibility dynamic that will cause you to live in a position of faithful stewardship?

2. Look at the three Energy and Responsibility bar graphs. Which of the three (Mythical Balance, Corrupted Energy, or Faithful Stewardship) most accurately describes where you are right now?

3. In the empty space below draw a bar graph reflecting the current relationship between your energy and responsibility.

4. Do you have more energy than responsibility? What are some areas of service you can invest in to carry more weight? It might be helpful to revisit the Concern vs. Responsibility diagram to see if you are ignoring any responsibilities.

5. Do you have more Responsibility than Energy? Who do you need to talk with to see if you are spending your energy on the right things? How was the gap created? How are you managing it? Are you relying on yourself and collapsing under the weight? Or are you relying on God and the community of faith to help you fill the gap?

08

PEACEBREAKERS, PEACEKEEPERS, AND PEACEMAKERS

An open rebuke is better than hidden love. Wounds from a sincere friend are better than many kisses from an enemy.

Proverbs 27:5-6

It's confession time. There are days I would rather lie to you than tell you the truth. It would be so much easier! Sometimes speaking truth is just downright hard. I want people to like me. I don't want to risk conflict; it makes me uncomfortable. And we already established comfort is an idol for me. It's not that I want to intentionally deceive you with outright lies, I just don't want to offend you. So I'm tempted to withhold truth; which is the same as lying. I would rather avoid and evade than do the heart-work required—fighting through layers of self-protection, fears, insecurities, desires, selfish motives—in order to speak the truth in love.

I've participated in and observed thousands of conversations between women, and I have come to the conclusion that we have two conversational tendencies with one another. We either act as a *peace-*

keeper or a *peacebreaker*. It's likely we lean more toward one or the other, though we are equally capable of both. More often than not, I would identify myself as a peacekeeper. That sounds so much sweeter than being a peacebreaker, doesn't it?! But Jesus didn't say "Blessed are the peace*keepers*." He said, "Blessed are the peace*makers*" (Matthew 5:11). So what's the difference?

In this chapter, we will explore the differences between three conversational tendencies: peacemaking, peacebreaking, and peacekeeping. Before we begin, take a look at the diagram to help understand their differences.

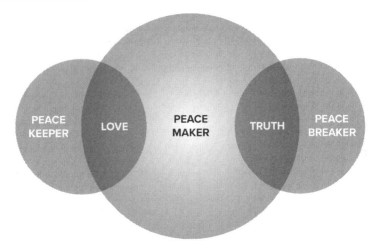

Peacekeeper, located on the left side of the diagram, errs toward love at the expense of truth.

Peacebreaker, located on the right side of the diagram, errs toward truth at the expense of love.

Peacemaker, located in the center, speaks both love and truth.

WHAT IS PEACE?

In order to gain clarity, we first need to understand how Scripture depicts peace. Peace is a robust and rich concept in Scripture, one that originates from and is rooted in God's own character. Peace is a key characteristic of who God is. He is a God of peace, who so desired peace with his people, that he acted in order to bring it about through Jesus, the Prince of Peace (Isaiah 9:6). God speaks peace to his people (Psalm 85:8) and sent prophets like John the Baptist who guided God's people along the path of peace (Luke 1:79). Jesus exhorted his disciples to be at peace with one another (Mark 9:50); a sentiment the apostle Paul echoed throughout his letters to the early churches. And in Jesus' farewell discourse, he told his disciples that though he was going away, he was leaving his peace with them (John 14:27) and he would send the Holy Spirit to be their helper and advocate (John 14:26), who would produce the fruit of peace in the lives of those who trust in him (Galatians 5:22). It is clear that peace is important to God and fundamental in the life of a believer.

What comes to mind when you think of peace? How would you define it? I think many people would define it as the absence of conflict or the presence of harmony, which is true. But that's only a dim shadow of biblical peace. In the Old Testament, peace is often connected to the idea of having one's physical needs met, having full relationships, being connected to community. [1] In the New Testament, the word for peace is *shalom*, which literally means uninjured, completeness, wholeness, welfare. [2] Wherever *shalom* is present there is well-being, abundance, wholeness, reconciliation. *Shalom* is the fruitful soil in which God's people flourish and grow in relation to him and to one another. God desires *shalom* for his people, individually and as a community.

The unfortunate reality is that we often misinterpret God's idea of flourishing as personal happiness and a life of comfort. But true *shalom* can't be disconnected from God's desire for justice and righteousness. According to associate professor Roberth Muthiah:

> While the Old Testament frames peace as a gift from God, it also calls for people to *embody* peace by seeking righteousness and confronting oppression and injustice. So peace

A WOMAN'S WORDS

isn't just a state of existence, [it] also has an ethical dimension. God's peace calls on us to *act* and *live* in corresponding ways." [3] *(emphasis author's own)*

With this understanding of peace in mind, we could describe a *peacemaker as an "ambassador of peace"—someone who ends wars by pursuing reconciliation, brings physical safety and health to people, seeks the well-being of others (spiritually, mentally, emotionally), and works to bring about justice in the world.* [4]

Ever since Genesis 3, God has been working toward full reconciliation with his people and total restoration of creation. He is reestablishing true *shalom* in all of creation, and the church is the epicenter of where this mission is accomplished. The church isn't an organization; the church is the people. And God uses broken people to minister to broken people. That's why Paul cared so much about the local church. In Ephesians 4, Paul gives us a vision into how God works through members of the local church to bring about peace.

Now these are the gifts Christ gave to the church: the apostles, the prophets, the evangelists, and the pastors and teachers. Their responsibility is to equip God's people to do his work and build up the church, the body of Christ. This will continue until we all come to such unity in our faith and knowledge of God's Son that *we will be mature in the Lord, measuring up to the full and complete standard of Christ.*

Then we will no longer be immature like children. We won't be tossed and blown about by every wind of new teaching. We will not be influenced when people try to trick us with lies so clever they sound like the truth. Instead, *we will speak the truth in love,* growing in every way more and more like Christ, who is the head of his body, the church. He makes the whole body fit together perfectly. As each part does its own special work, it helps the other parts grow, *so that the whole body is healthy and growing and full of love.*

Ephesians 4:11–16, *(emphasis author's own)*

Christ gave specific gifts to the local church: apostles, pastors, teachers, evangelists, and prophets. These are the men and women to whom God has entrusted his people. Their job is to teach and equip God's people—*you and me*—to do the work of ministry and build up the church. The work of ministering to one another, of encouraging one another in the faith, of calling one another to repentance and a life of faith, is not the work of a handful of church workers. It's the calling of every man and woman who believes in Jesus Christ. And Paul says we must continue to labor in this work until we become mature in the Lord, measuring up to the full and complete standard of Christ.

When Paul speaks of maturity in this passage, a picture of *shalom* emerges. Maturity indicates something is full-grown, complete in all its parts, perfect. [5] Paul says if we are faithful in the work of ministering to one another and helping one another grow in maturity, then we will be firmly grounded in sound doctrine, we will speak the truth in love to one another, and we will grow in every way more like Christ. All of this happens as each part—*you and me*—do the work God has entrusted to us, which helps the other parts grow. In essence, *shalom* is restored and the whole body of Christ is flourishing—or as Paul said, it is healthy and growing and full of love. What a beautiful picture of the *shalom* of God! And we get to participate with God in the work of restoring *shalom*, restoring peace on earth.

Making peace, being agents of peace in the world, means we seek the well-being (spiritual, mental, physical, emotional) of others in our interactions with them—including the words we speak and the deeds we enact. For the purpose of this study, however, we will explore the idea of peacemaking only through the words we speak.

TRUTH AND LOVE

Peacemaking is a responsibility of the believer—one I think is clearly seen in Jesus' message to the early churches in the book of Revelation. He has a message for each of them—one we can learn from even two thousand years later. To the church in Ephesus, Jesus says:

> I know all the things you do. I have seen your hard work and your patient endurance. I know you don't tolerate evil people. You have examined the claims of those who say they are apostles but are not. You have discovered they are liars. You have patiently suffered for me without quitting.
>
> But I have this complaint against you. You don't love me or each other as you did at first! Look how far you have fallen! Turn back to me and do the works you did at first. If you don't repent, I will come and remove your lampstand from its place among the churches. But this is in your favor: You hate the evil deeds of the Nicolaitans, just as I do.
>
> Revelation 2:2–6

The church in Ephesus was working, toiling, striving, enduring, and spending themselves on behalf of the gospel. They also hated and did not tolerate the evil deeds of the Nicolaitans. And Jesus commended them for this. But, he said, they had no love. They didn't love each other, nor did they love Jesus as when they first believed. For all of their good works, for all of the steadfast resolve against sin, they still lacked something Jesus views as vital and necessary in his church—*love*.

Jesus had a similar message to the church in Thyatira,

> I know all the things you do. I have seen your love, your faith, your service, and your patient endurance. And I can see your constant improvement in all these things.

But I have this complaint against you. You are permitting that woman—that Jezebel who calls herself a prophet—to lead my servants astray. She teaches them to commit sexual sin and to eat food offered to idols. I gave her time to repent, but she does not want to turn away from her immorality.

Therefore, I will throw her on a bed of suffering, and those who commit adultery with her will suffer greatly unless they repent and turn away from her evil deeds. I will strike her children dead. Then all the churches will know that I am the one who searches out the thoughts and intentions of every person. And I will give to each of you whatever you deserve.

Revelation 2:19-23

The church in Thyatira was full of love, faith, and service. Jesus commended them for this. But they were tolerating sin and allowing evil to dwell among them. For all of their love and faith, they too lacked something Jesus views as vital and necessary in his church—*truth.*

One church was all love and no truth, and he called them to repent. The other church was all truth and no love, and he called them to repent as well. *Love and truth should not exist apart from one another.* If you love someone more than yourself, you will tell them the truth. But if you tell them the truth without love, then you aren't really loving them at all. True lovers of peace must also be lovers of righteousness. Love and truth go hand in hand. This is seen very clearly in the person and work of Jesus Christ. Love and truth are not in opposition. Jesus did not pit them against one another, nor should we. Jesus Christ was full of grace and truth (John 1:14).

Both peacekeeping and peacebreaking lack the real hope and power of the gospel to advance the peace of God in the world. But Jesus had another message, one of commendation and future glory. There were some members of the church in Thyatira who were true peacemakers—they exhibited love, faith, and service like the rest of the church at

LOVE AND TRUTH

SHOULD NOT EXIST APART

FROM ONE ANOTHER.

Thyatira—but they also held firm to the truth of Scripture, and had not given themselves to false teaching. And Jesus commended them and made a great promise to them, if they endured:

> But I also have a message for the rest of you in Thyatira who have not followed this false teaching ('deeper truths,' as they call them—depths of Satan, actually). I will ask nothing more of you except that you hold tightly to what you have until I come. To all who are victorious, who obey me to the very end,
>
> To them I will give authority over all the nations.
>
> They will rule the nations with an iron rod
>
> and smash them like clay pots.
>
> They will have the same authority I received from my Father, and I will also give them the morning star!
>
> Revelation 2:24-28

I cannot fathom the magnitude of Jesus' statement to the faithful in Thyatira. He will give them the same authority he received from the Father. They will rule the nations and he will give them the morning star. What glory awaits those who remain faithful to the end!

Questions for Reflection

1. Is your conversational tendency to speak more love or more truth?

2. In Jesus' message to the churches, he delivered both a commendation and a rebuke. As you examine your conversational tendencies, what commendation and rebuke would Jesus have for you?

PEACEMAKING

So what does it look like to be a peacemaker? *Where peacebreaking is the truth without love, and peacekeeping love without truth, true biblical peacemaking is speaking the truth in love.*

Peacemaking is not just the absence of conflict or trouble; it is the presence of everything that makes for our greatest good. Jesus is called the Prince of Peace. He didn't sacrifice or compromise the truth so others would like him. He spoke the truth boldly. But he was kind and compassionate and full of love. Jesus was both tough and tender. Timothy Keller once said,

> Love without truth is sentimentality; it supports and affirms us but keeps us in denial about our flaws. Truth without love is harshness; it gives us information but in such a way that we cannot really hear it. God's saving love in Christ, however, is marked by both radical truthfulness about who we are and yet also radical, unconditional commitment to us. The merciful commitment strengthens us to see the truth about ourselves and repent. The conviction and repentance moves us to cling to and rest in God's mercy and grace. [6]

This is the heart of peacemaking. Peacemaking includes speaking both truth *and* love. God's true prophets spoke God's words even when it meant they would not be popular. They spoke God's warnings and rebukes even when it meant they would suffer isolation from the community. Jesus spoke the truth, knowing he would die for it. The apostles and members of the early church continued to affirm and speak truth and many of them were stoned. They didn't protect themselves nor promote themselves. They spoke only of Christ crucified. They spoke of God's love, grace, and forgiveness of sin but not apart from the importance of confession, repentance, and faithful obedience. Peacemaking is more than empty words, empty wishes, or empty encouragement. Being agents of peace is costly.

The apostle Paul went to great lengths to live this out. His life's mission was to share not only the hope held out in the gospel, but also to exhort, rebuke, train, and instruct the new believers and early churches. All of Paul's letters to the churches contained rebuke for their specific sins and encouragement in godliness. And nearing the end of his ministry, Paul had one final message for the elders of the church in Ephesus.

> You know that from the day I set foot in the province of Asia until now I have done the Lord's work humbly and with many tears. I have endured the trials that came to me from the plots of the Jews. *I never shrank back from telling you what you needed to hear,* either publicly or in your homes. I have had one message for Jews and Greeks alike—the necessity of repenting from sin and turning to God, and of having faith in our Lord Jesus . . I declare today that I have been faithful. If anyone suffers eternal death, it's not my fault, for *I didn't shrink from declaring all that God wants you to know.*
>
> Acts 20:18-21, 26-27 *(emphasis author's own)*

Paul, in his final message to them, wanted them to know that he had been faithful to them and never shrank back from telling them all they needed to hear. This was so important to him he said it twice. Paul took full responsibility in his mission as an ambassador of Christ—faithfully declaring the gospel and instructing believers in lives of obedience. And he often did so at great cost to himself—suffering at the hands of those who rejected his message, accused him unjustly, and slandered him and his ministry. But no matter what, he did not fail to tell the people all God wanted them to know. He did not miss an opportunity to encourage people in obedience. He never changed his message, regardless of the potential cost.

True peacemaking is founded on trust in God that alleviates our fear of man and need for the approval of others. It is rooted in humility, not moral superiority; and it is full of love and compassion. As Christians, we are called to spur one another on toward spiritual maturity, to encourage one another in perseverance and faithfulness. We are to pursue what makes for peace and mutual upbuilding (Romans 14:19 ESV). Peacemaking builds others up, not in a superficial way, but in a way that helps them grow strong. We are helping others build a wall of righteousness, stepping into the gaps and helping repair the breaches. And they are to do the same thing for us. We are to help fortify and strengthen one another in the battle against sin and to pursue the *shalom* that God has for his people. James said that peacemakers who sow seeds of peace will reap a harvest of righteousness (James 3:18). Ultimately, peacemaking glorifies God and strengthens and unifies his church.

We are each other's eyes and ears. Sin is so insidious and deceptive. I can become utterly convinced that something is a great idea. I can rationalize and justify almost anything in my head. I need people who are committed to walk alongside me, people who are more concerned about my holiness and spiritual life than they are about my temporal happiness. I need people who are committed to furthering the kingdom of God on earth and helping me look more like Jesus. I need people who are willing to discomfort themselves on my behalf. People who are willing to risk tension because they love me.

Question for Reflection

A peacemaker will speak both truth and love. Here are some examples of what true peacemaking speech looks like. *As you look over this list, identify any of the examples below that describe the way you use your words, or how others would say you use your words.*

PEACEMAKING SPEECH

- Speaks gentle, but unwavering words of rebuke, correction, and truth
- Tough, but tender
- FOR the other person
- Believes the best of others, rather than being quick to assume, judge, or believe the worst
- Others-focused
- Thoughtful and intentional
- Seeks the true well-being of others
- Promotes holiness and righteousness
- Corrects, teaches, instructs, reasons, admonishes
- Encourages—builds others up on truth not flattery
- Genuinely loves others
- Quick to overlook insignificant offenses
- Peaceable
- Pursues reconciliation even when wounded by the other
- Does not compromise or withhold the truth in order to preserve the relationship

- Highest goal is helping others grow in Christ-likeness
- Embraces the sometimes difficult task of seeking others highest good
- Sacrificial
- Rooted in humility, sees oneself as the chief of sinners and approaches others from this mentality
- Is sincere, respectful, and approachable
- Listens to others and is quick to see from another's point of view
- Gives grace to hearers

The problem, though, is our words travel through our own broken conversational tendencies and we miss opportunities to speak true peace. So as we seek to grow in stewarding our words, we need to identify a few of peace's counterfeits: *peacekeeping and peacebreaking.*

PEACEKEEPING

Peacekeeping is eerily similar to the false prophets in the Old Testament, who failed to call Israel to repentance and warn of his coming judgment. Instead they led the people of Israel to a false sense of security. The false prophets spoke what the people wanted to hear, rather than what they needed to hear. They lulled God's people into a spiritual slumber—speaking words that at worst led them astray, or at best left them blissfully ignorant of their sin and rebellion. They gave assurances of peace where there was no peace and they offered God's people superficial treatments for their mortal wounds (Jeremiah 6:13–14). In effect, they were treating a gunshot wound with a Band-Aid. The people of God were bleeding out in their sin and rebellion, and no one was willing to speak the truth to one another.

The false prophets failed to love the people of God for the glory of God. They didn't call them to lives of holiness. Instead, they sought honor, popularity, and favor among the people. They tickled the people's ears with things they wanted to hear. They sought their own glory and good, their own comfort and security. They abandoned God's people and God's mission in favor of self-preservation.

This same issue is alive and well in our society and in our churches today. Far too often we fail to live in true biblical fellowship with one another. We are either unwilling or afraid to speak the truth to one another. We see danger ahead for our brothers and sisters, but we whitewash it with empty platitudes or false assurances of peace. We say things like, "Who am I to judge?" as if that frees us from our responsibility toward one another. We affirm one another's right to be happy. And all the while, we watch as others bleed out in their sin and rebellion—failing to step into the gap and call one another to live lives marked by confession and repentance of sin and faithful obedience to the Lord. We hear words like obedience and repentance and cry, "legalism" and instead speak grace over mortal wounds. We view our peacekeeping tendencies as good, when in reality they are cowardly and self-protective. We are no different than the false prophets who declared, "Peace, peace" where there was no peace.

A woman who struggles with peacekeeping has a hard time telling others the truth. She doesn't want to hurt anyone's feelings. Rather than providing important feedback she opts for flattery instead. The fear of angering others, being rejected, or the possibility of losing the relationship drives her. She places high value on the relationships in her life, which isn't necessarily a bad thing, unless it hinders her from being obedient to God and speaking truth to others, even if it means creating tension in the relationship.

This is an area of struggle for me. I want comfort and ease. I want to be liked, and I don't like conflict. God has helped me grow in this area over the last several years, but there are still a few relationships where I have to work hard to be truthful. For example, in one specific relationship, I have to make a conscious effort to be truthful because I don't want to lose her friendship or risk conflict. In a recent conversation, she was discussing a situation in her life that concerned me. I was fairly confident she was self-deceived and blinded by her desires and, as a result, wasn't making wise choices. I was also sure that continuing on this path could be harmful to her and to others. But because of our friendship, the temptation to remain silent was strong. I didn't want to outright lie or encourage her choices, but I struggled to discourage them, which is just as bad. To do this is to choose myself and what I want (a tension-free relationship with my friend) over her greater good and overall well-being.

Peacekeeping is sticking your head in the sand and ignoring the fact that your friend is, knowingly or unknowingly, speeding toward a cliff. It's a subtle form of dishonesty, withholding the truth and critical feedback that could be helpful. Sometimes we don't speak because we aren't sure or we lack clarity, which isn't wrong. But we often have more clarity than we allow ourselves to believe. A good way to know is if we are clearer outside of the room than we are inside of the room. If you find yourself discussing your friend's situation with others with greater clarity than you discussed it with your friend, then you are lying and functioning as a peacekeeper. This is to the detriment of everyone involved.

Peacekeeping is not what Christ desires from us. He desires us to love him, first and foremost, and then to love one another as we would love ourselves (Leviticus 19:18; Mark 12:31). He desires that we help one another, encourage one another, and protect one another against temptation, attack, and hard times.

Questions for Reflection

As we seek to identify and repent of our peacekeeping tendencies, it might be helpful to look at some common characteristics of peacekeeping. *Identify any of the examples below that describe the way you use your words, or how others would say you use your words.*

PEACEKEEPING SPEECH

- Passive
- Self-protective
- Compromises on the truth
- Reluctant to talk about sin with others
- Avoids conflict
- Appeases others
- Focuses on being nice
- Wants people to like them
- Withholds the truth, skirts the truth, or shares only partial truth
- verly deferential to others
- Would rather preserve a relationship with someone than risk losing it by speaking hard truth
- More focused on their own comfort and security than the overall good of others
- Apprehensive about confrontation
- Overly agreeable
- Flatters
- Often says, "I don't want to hurt their feelings"
- Indifferent
- Apathetic

- Expresses selfish non-disturbance
- Selfishly unconcerned

1. Where have you avoided confrontation, leaving issues unre-solved and/or relationships unreconciled? Why?

2. Have you ever had insight or wisdom pertaining to someone's life but avoided sharing it with them? Why?

3. Have you ever said, "Who am I to judge?" or "I'm not their Holy Spirit" as a way of avoiding speaking into someone's life? Why?

4. Has anyone ever spoken hard truth to you? How did their will-ingness to speak help you?

PEACEBREAKING

Where peacekeeping is spiritually impotent and lacks power, peacebreaking is spiritually oppressive. If peacekeeping is love without truth, peacebreaking is truth without love. Where peacekeeping is rooted in fear of man, peacebreaking is rooted in a feeling of moral superiority. Peacekeepers are typically more reluctant to address someone's sin due to an excessive desire to be liked or preserve the relationship, while peacebreakers may eagerly call out sin in others. *Peacekeeping leads to a church that is weak, frail, and vulnerable. Peacebreaking leads to a church that is fractured, wounded, and calloused.*

Sometimes we degenerate into quarrels that disrupt the *shalom* God intends. Not all conflict is bad. In fact, sometimes conflict is necessary and can be handled in ways to help others move toward true *shalom*. But if conflict is not, first and foremost, rooted in love, fruitful, or redemptive, then it is disruptive to the body of Christ and to the work God has for us to do. This is at the heart of Paul's plea to two women in Philippi:

> Now I appeal to Euodia and Syntyche. Please, because you belong to the Lord, settle your disagreement. And I ask you, my true partner, to help these two women, for they worked hard with me in telling others the Good News. They worked along with Clement and the rest of my co-workers, whose names are written in the Book of Life.

> Philippians 4:2-3

Euodia and Syntyche had labored alongside Paul, Clement, and the rest of Paul's coworkers to spread the good news of the gospel. They had at one time been united in their love of Christ and in the work of ministry, but something had come between them and word of their disagreement had reached Paul, who wrote this letter while he was in prison. Literally, Paul pleads with them to "be of the same mind in the Lord."

Then he pleads with his "true partner" to assist these women in ending their conflict. Though Paul is in prison, he is deeply concerned about the division between these two women and wants to make sure they resolve their conflict and continue on in the work of the Lord.

If you were to survey non-Christians today and ask them what they think about Christians, many would say we are an unkind, judgmental people. We are known more by what we are against than what we are for. This reminds me of a TED Talk by a young woman named Megan Phelps-Roper, a former member of a controversial church well-known for the harsh and hateful ways it speaks against those who believe differently. After a few people, particularly one young Jewish man who later became her husband, engaged Megan in thoughtful and civil dialogue regarding her beliefs, she began to see the error of her ways and eventually left the church. Roper, describing her journey in a TED Talk said, "I learned not to care how my manner of speaking affected others. I thought my rightness justified my rudeness—harsh tones, raised voices, insults, interruptions—but that strategy is ultimately counterproductive. Dialing up the volume and the snark is natural in stressful situations, but it tends to bring the conversation to an unsatisfactory, explosive end." [7]

The essence of peacebreaking is a failure to feel empathy and compassion for the person you are speaking to. Because you aren't concerned with what others think about you, you don't find it difficult to speak your mind. *But rightness doesn't justify rudeness.* Deep, abiding, Christ-like love for others should always temper our words. Watching Roper's video caused me to wonder how many times I have been certain of my rightness, and spoke in a way that was critical and harsh and, as a result, counterproductive.

When we degenerate into conflict over personal or personality preferences, we weaken the church and the message of the gospel loses its power and appeal to the outside world. When we fall under the assumption that our "rightness justifies our rudeness," we ruin oppor-

WE NEED A NEW HEART, NEW DESIRES, AND A NEW NATURE. ONLY A NEW MAN CAN LIVE A NEW LIFE. BUT THE GOOD NEWS IS THAT, IF YOUR HOPE IS IN JESUS AND HIS WORK ON YOUR BEHALF, YOU ARE INDEED NEW.

tunities for the gospel to go forth. When we bite and devour, we crush others with our words rather than strengthen them.

This is a matter deeply concerning to both Paul and Peter, who often urged believers to be united in the faith—a unity also displayed through how we love one another *in* conflict. Remember, conflict is not necessarily a bad thing. The issue is do we engage one another well and in ways that promote true *shalom*? Our job as agents of peace is to seek and promote righteousness and confront issues of oppression or injustice. Paul never shied away from this. He was fiercely committed to telling the truth, calling out sin, and exhorting believers to "live in a manner worthy of the gospel" (Philippians 1:27). But he did so with the deep, abiding love for those he confronted. Paul began many of his letters reminding the believers how he longed to help them grow strong in the Lord, how he never stopped praying for them, how he thanked God for them, and how he loved and longed for them with the affection of Christ (Romans 1:8–12; Philippians 1:3–11). His love always preceded truth, direction, and correction.

Many of us give into our sinful conversational tendencies as peace-breakers, rather than thoughtfully and purposefully speaking as a peacemaker. We push our own agendas. We love our rightness more than God's righteousness. We live as if it is our job to humble others, rather than humble ourselves. We hold others to our beliefs and standards and punish them with our words when they don't. Rather than promote true peace, we are disruptive, combative, and argumentative. We do this in our marriages, workplaces, neighborhoods, and peer groups. And with the ease of online engagement, we vocalize it on social media apart from the context of community, the breeding ground for true, biblical peacemaking.

Peacebreaking may also be rooted in a feeling of moral superiority and self-righteousness. We are more concerned with correcting others' flawed thinking and actions. This often leads to fractured relationships, churches, communities, and families. Jesus warned against this in Matthew:

Do not judge others, and you will not be judged. For you will be treated as you treat others. The standard you use in judging is the standard by which you will be judged. And why worry about a speck in your friend's eye when you have a log in your own? How can you think of saying to your friend, 'Let me help you get rid of that speck in your eye,' when you can't see past the log in your own eye? Hypocrite! First get rid of the log in your own eye; then you will see well enough to deal with the speck in your friend's eye.

Matthew 7:1-5

Jesus' concern is not as much that we judge one another, it's that we don't judge one another rightly. All too often we judge one another from a place of moral superiority, rather than in love and humility, considering others as better than ourselves. This kind of judgement isn't redemptive or profitable. It doesn't advance peace; it hinders it. Peacebreaking is spiritually oppressive. It is speaking the truth without love, which is brutality. Truth without love is harsh. It crushes people; it tears them down.

Jesus' exhortation is that we first look at the log in our own eyes—the depths of our own brokenness and sin. We need to form a right estimate of ourselves first. Then and only then will we be able to form a right estimate about our friend's issue and speak to them in a way that promotes peace. When a woman knows and understands the depths of her own brokenness and sin, she will exhibit great humility in her dealings with others. She doesn't rejoice in pointing out sin in another person, but does so with great sorrow and reverence for the person with whom she is engaged.

Questions for Reflection

As we seek to identify and repent of our peacebreaking tendencies, it might be helpful to look at some common characteristics of peacebreaking. *Identify any of the examples below that describe the way you use your words, or how others would say you use them.*

PEACEBREAKING SPEECH

- Inflammatory
- Condemning
- Adversarial
- Aggressive
- Quarrelsome
- Argumentative
- Quick to correct others or point out their sin
- Antagonistic
- Combative
- Unyielding
- Critical/Fault-finding
- Oppositional
- Needs to be right
- Lacks empathy
- Self-righteous
- Hypocritical
- Asserts personal rights
- Proud/Arrogant
- Judgmental
- Contentious

- Nagging
- Harsh
- Unkind

1. Have you ever been described as a bully? If so, why do you think that may be?

2. What tactics do you use with others when trying to get your own way?

3. Do others feel safe being vulnerable around you? Or do they often feel criticized?

4. When in conflict with others, what is something you hear over and over again (i.e. "You never listen" or "You always have to be right")? If you are not sure, make an effort to pay attention to how people respond to you.

5. Discuss a time when you dealt harshly with someone, telling them what you thought they needed to hear, but not in genuine love and goodwill. Did it fracture or promote true peace? How so?

SO WHAT ARE WE SUPPOSED TO DO?

First, identify your conversational tendency. Let's look at the diagram again:

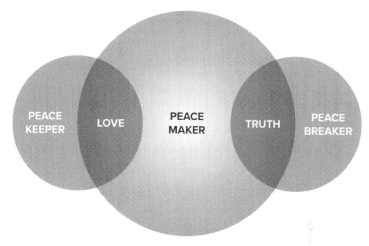

Are you more of a peacekeeper or a peacebreaker? If you aren't sure, ask someone close to you to help provide clarity.

If you are a *peacebreaker*, know that your tendency may be to *sacrifice love in favor of truth*. Before you speak to someone, pause. Take time to pray and consider not just the words you speak, but also your delivery and timing. Place yourself in the other's shoes long enough to determine how to best approach them. You may be blunt and direct and prefer people to speak to you in ways that are blunt and direct, but remember not everyone is the same. Also, not every situation is the same. Some days, when your friend is anxious, remember "a gentle answer deflects anger, but harsh words make tempers flare" (Proverbs 15:1). In moments like this, a gentle word of encouragement over a stern rebuke goes a long way. But on another day, if your friend is proud and in a repeated pattern of rebellion and chaos, a firm word may be necessary. The point is we must ask the Lord to temper our speech according to what our friend most needs. Pray for the Lord to free you from selfish and self-centered ideas like "this is just how God made me" and "I am just a person who speaks my mind; at least people know where they stand with me." Instead of expecting others to accept you as you are, pray that the Lord would grant you compassion and understanding so you can meet others where they are. Pray that he would allow you to love those in your life with his love, and as a result bring him great glory and make his love visible in the world.

If you are a *peacekeeper*, know your tendency may be to *sacrifice truth in favor of love*. Because of this, it will take more effort on your part to speak words of truth. Don't neglect an opportunity to love those in your life with words of truth. Remember, "a bold reproof promotes peace" (Proverbs 10:10b). Truth leads to life and freedom. Also don't run from the good, heart-work that can be done in you. It takes a lot of courage to speak the truth. When you take a step in faith and obedience, doing the unnatural and hard thing, God uses it to grow and mature you in remarkable ways. Pray that the Lord would help you love the people in your life more than you need them. God did not give us a spirit of fear and timidity, but one of power, love, and self-discipline (2 Timothy 1:7). Pray that he would instill and mature this spirit in you, that you would be able to speak the truth in love and with bold humility.

Remember, this won't come naturally. In fact, we will often fail because it goes against our natural tendencies. We need a new heart, new desires, and a new nature. Only a new man can live a new life. But the good news is that, if your hope is in Jesus and his work on your behalf, you are indeed new. Paul assures us if we let the Holy Spirit guide our lives, we won't do what our sinful nature desires (Galatians 5:16). We can pray for the Spirit to produce his fruit in us, to give us new desires, and to mold us into the image and likeness of Christ, who is the Prince of Peace. We don't have to do this in our own wisdom or strength because the Holy Spirit, the same power who raised Jesus from the dead, lives in us. The good news is as we draw near to Christ, and seek the direction and power of the Holy Spirit, the fruit of our lives will more naturally begin to reflect Christ's character in both our words and actions. Jesus not only made peace possible; he makes it possible for us to be peacemakers.

09

CLEAN LIPS

And whatever you do or say, do it as a representative of the Lord Jesus, giving thanks through him to God the Father.

Colossians 3:17

As we have seen in Scripture, our words are a mixture of blessing and cursing, of life and death. If we desire to be women who fulfill God's call on our lives, we need to cry out to the Lord and ask him to transform our speech.

This exactly what the prophet Isaiah did near the beginning of his ministry. In an equally awesome and terrifying moment, Isaiah saw the Lord in all his majesty. He stood in the presence of the holy God, witnessing unbelievably magnificent and holy things. So awesome, so incredible was this sight that Isaiah became acutely aware of his sinfulness. Ironically, the sin Isaiah felt compelled to confess in that moment was not about reading Scripture more or going to the temple more often; the sin Isaiah was woefully aware of in the sight of God was the sinfulness of his words, his unclean lips (Isaiah 6:1–5). One of the winged creatures responded to Isaiah's confession by picking up a burning coal from the altar and touching it to Isaiah's lips, declaring he had been forgiven and cleansed of his sin. Then, hearing the Lord call out, "Whom should I send as a messenger to this people? Who will go for us?" Isaiah immediately responded, "Here I am. Send me." (Isaiah 6:6–8). You can almost feel his excitement. Like a kid raising his hand saying, "Pick me! Pick me!"

The Lord had a mission for Isaiah; he was looking for a messenger, a mouthpiece—someone who would proclaim the very words of God to the people of Israel. Before that could happen though, there needed to be a symbolic cleansing to indicate the forgiveness of Isaiah's sins. Isaiah knew the hypocrisy of his own speech. How could he speak the words of God to people in deep need when his own words flowed from unclean lips! So in his great mercy, the Lord applied the purifying fire to Isaiah's lips—the place where Isaiah identified his greatest sin and need and ironically, the place where God intended to use Isaiah most profoundly to become one of his most prolific prophets—calling Judah and Jerusalem to repentance and faith in the Lord, speaking words of life, should they choose to hear and obey.

As the church, as members of the body of Christ, we have a mission similar to Isaiah. We have a responsibility to call one another to faithfulness, obedience and repentance. God uses us to sharpen, encourage, rebuke, and instruct one another. The author of Hebrews exhorted believers to this end:

> Be careful then, dear brothers and sisters. Make sure that your own hearts are not evil and unbelieving, turning you away from the living God. You must warn each other every day, while it is still "today," so that none of you will be deceived by sin and hardened against God. For if we are faithful to the end, trusting God just as firmly as when we first believed, we will share in all that belongs to Christ.
>
> Hebrews 3:12–14

We are to serve one another in love, being each other's eyes and ears. We are called to *speak*, exhorting one another daily so no one will be deceived and lured away by their sinful desires and actions. We are to partner with others, to own their cause in such a way that we are working for their ultimate good. As women created in the image of God—entrusted with his *ezer* nature to be a source of strength and aid—and as followers of Jesus, we have an important message to share with one another and with the world around us. We have a message of hope and life for anyone who chooses to hear and heed—the message of who God is, what he is doing in the world, and what he has done for us through Christ. These are the words of eternal life, and God in his unfathomable kindness allows us to be speakers of this message.

But because both blessing and cursing come pouring out of our mouths (James 3:10), many will not listen to us. They see the hypocrisy and duplicity of our lives—declaring ourselves to be Christians and proclaiming the truths of Scripture, while at the same time judgment, slander, derogatory comments, racial slurs, and gossip flow from our lips. If we hope to be effective messengers of God's grace, mercy, truth, and blessing to the world around us, we need the Lord to purify our lips from speech not befitting those created in the image of God and redeemed by the blood of Christ. We need our speech to be renewed and transformed so it may reflect the *ezer* nature the Lord entrusted to us.

Question for Reflection

1. Like Isaiah, we need to get to a place where we can say, "Woe is me, I am a woman of unclean lips." Until we are aware of our sin and brokenness nothing changes. Awareness and confession precede repentance. What specific areas of unbelief and sin has this study exposed? Take some time to process what God has shown you and move toward confession and repentance. If you are unwilling, why are you hesitant?

WORSHIP TRANSFORMS OUR DESIRES

Isaiah's transformational experience began with worship. *Our transformation also begins with worship.* We were created for worship. Because we were created for worship, our hearts *will* worship something. The question is who or what will we worship?

Over the last several chapters, we have explored our propensity to worship the wrong things. We turn comfort, approval, power, justice, control, gratification, and glory into functional gods and worship them instead of the one true God. We worship the lesser, rather than the One who is able to do immeasurably more than we could ever ask or imagine (Ephesians 3:20).

> If we consider the unblushing promises of reward and the staggering nature of the rewards promised in the Gospels, it would seem that Our Lord finds our desires not too strong, but too weak. We are half-hearted creatures, fooling about with drink and sex and ambition when infinite joy is offered us, like an ignorant child who wants to go on making mud pies in a slum because he cannot imagine what is meant by the offer of a holiday at the sea. *We are far too easily pleased.*
>
> C.S. Lewis, *The Weight of Glory* [1]

The problem isn't that our desires are bad, it's that we are settling for an inferior substitute.

Let's look back to the tree illustration. Trees need water to survive. Their roots grow deep and wide in search of water. It doesn't matter if they find toxic water in a sewer or the slightest droplets in a broken cistern. Just like the tree, we need water to survive, and our hearts will seek it wherever it can be found. When we settle for drinking water from the sewer our roots become diseased and produce diseased fruit.

The prophet Jeremiah illustrates this for us:

Cursed are those who put their trust in mere humans who rely on human strength and turn their hearts away from the Lord. They are like stunted shrubs in the desert, with no hope for the future. They will live in the barren wilderness, in an uninhabited salty land.

Jeremiah 17:5-6

When we turn away from worshiping the one true God and, in our autonomy, seek life in our functional gods of control, comfort, approval, security, power, gratification, justice, and glory, we will be like a shrub in the desert—barren, withered, and parched.

But Jeremiah continues:

But blessed are those who trust in the Lord and have made the Lord their hope and confidence. They are like trees planted along a riverbank, with roots that reach deep into the water. Such trees are not bothered by the heat or worried by long months of drought. Their leaves stay green, and they never stop producing fruit.

Jeremiah 17:7-8

The difference between the withered tree and the fruitful tree is who or what you trust in, where you are seeking life. When Jesus meets the Samaritan woman at the well in John 4, he tells her he is living water and if she drinks of him she will never thirst again. If we will drink from the living water Jesus holds out to us, we will find all our desires fulfilled in him.

When we turn our hearts back to the Lord, he doesn't replace our desire for comfort with something else, he becomes our comfort. He doesn't replace our desire for approval, he fulfills it. He tells us we are already accepted and approved in him. He doesn't replace our desire for control; he promises he is in control of all things and so we can rest. He doesn't replace our desire for power; he purifies it and manifests his power through us. He doesn't replace our desire for gratification, he satisfies us. He doesn't stop our desire for justice, he promises justice is accomplished in Christ. He doesn't replace our desire for glory; he promises we will be transformed into his image with ever-increasing glory (2 Corinthians 3:18). Jesus transforms all of our desires by satisfying us with himself and with the work he has accomplished and will accomplish. As a result, our gaze shifts from our insufficiency to his all-sufficiency and our worship shifts from ourselves back to him who alone is worthy of worship. This is fruitful ground for transformed speech to take root.

Questions for Reflection

1. Think about your idol—your functional god. In what ways is God enough to meet that need and satisfy that desire? Be specific. Write it down. If you really believe it, how will it transform your worship? How will it transform your speech?

2. The transformation of our speech begins when we realize Christ is sufficient; he alone is enough. We will need daily reminders of this because our hearts are prone to wander. We have to keep going back to the well that will never run dry. What are some practical ways you can begin to drink deeply of what Christ is offering you instead of running to a broken cistern that holds no water?

JESUS TRANSFORMS OUR

DESIRES BY SATISFYING US

WITH HIMSELF. AS A RESULT,

OUR GAZE SHIFTS FROM OUR

INSUFFICIENCY TO HIS ALL

SUFFICIENCY AND OUR WORSHIP

SHIFTS FROM OURSELVES

BACK TO HIM.

TRANSFORMED SPEECH

I've met some remarkable women in my life—smart, accomplished, powerful, driven. But some of the most amazing women I've had the privilege to know are servants, women who give their lives away. They become poorer, weakened, and tired so others find strength, hope, and refreshment. I've been blessed to be nurtured by several of these women in my lifetime. Each is unique with vastly different strengths and personalities. But when I think of how they've used their words with me, commonalities emerge. Each woman provided me with a place of refuge, a safe place to wrestle through whatever issues I had. They provided me with respite, wisdom, encouragement, and truth—so much truth. They didn't withhold truth that would be beneficial to me—even if it hurt. Each delivered life-giving truth with grace, tenderhearted mercy, and loving-kindness. And I could receive it because I knew beyond a shadow of a doubt each one of them knew me, loved me, and was *for* me. Some days they delivered words of affirmation, other days they delivered words of correction. Some days they pushed me out of my comfort zone and challenged me to do hard things, and other days they comforted me and used words to restore peace in my mind and heart. They weren't harsh or critical or judgmental. They were the living, breathing embodiment of Proverbs 31:26, "When she speaks, her words are wise, and she gives instructions with kindness." Their words shaped, refined, encouraged, and protected me (often from myself). They didn't just want to affirm me and make me feel good about myself, because they knew that wasn't what would help me most. I am who I am, in large part, because these women committed to loving me with their words. This is the beauty and power of redeemed speech.

An introverted or quiet woman might be tempted to feel this isn't possible for her to do. But redemptive speech is not about being eloquent or extroverted; it's not personality-dependent. Some of the women who impacted me were incredibly gifted with words, others stumbled and struggled to find the right words. Some were outspoken and bold in their speech, while others were reserved and quiet. But they all were equally faithful in using their words to help me grow in spiritual maturity. This is something every woman can do regardless of her personality or gifting. It just looks different for each woman. The goal is faithfulness, not perfection—being willing to use words in ways that encourage others in their faith journey. We want to be women committed to loving others through our speech.

The transformation of our speech is possible because of the finished work of Christ. The apostle Paul taught that the work of Christ should inform not only our beliefs, but also our actions. Paul urged the Ephesians, as those who now belonged to Christ, to throw off their old sinful nature and former way of life. Living according to their old ways no longer fit them—it wasn't consistent with who God created them to be. They had a new nature. If we think back to the tree illustration, the fruit is native to the tree; it matches. So a fig tree produces figs and an apple tree produces apples. A fig tree can't produce apples. They don't match. Just like figs aren't native to an apple tree, lying, abusive and foul language, bitterness, rage, anger, harsh words, slander, and all types of evil behavior aren't native to the believer (Ephesians 4:17–24, Colossians 3:5–10).

Why? Because you have a new nature.

Because God chose us to be his beloved children, we should put on our new nature and clothe ourselves in tenderhearted mercy, humility, and kindness (Colossians 3:12). We are to use our words to teach and counsel one another with all the wisdom Christ has given and to sing psalms and hymns and spiritual songs (Colossians 3:12–16a). And, whatever we do or say, we are to "do it as a representative of the Lord Jesus, giving thanks through him to God the Father" (Colossians 3:16b–17). This is the fruit consistent with with a woman who has been made new in Christ.

Paul's words charging them to speak and live as Christ's representative are weighty, and we should take some time to reflect on the implications. To speak as someone's representative means your speech reflects their values, their desires, their character, their mission. This happens even within the Trinity itself—Jesus spoke only what the Father wanted him to say (John 12:49) and the Holy Spirit speaks only what he has heard (John 16:13). Their words are representative of God the Father, reflecting his heart, character, and mission. So too we, who have been adopted into the family of God and bear his name, are to speak and act in ways that are characteristic of Jesus.

Jesus' words, as recorded in Scripture, contain everything from rebuke to tenderhearted mercy. It didn't matter if he was admonishing the religious or comforting the downtrodden, the message was always the same—repent, believe, and find life. That message never changed—whether it was one of his closest friends or someone who vehemently opposed his ministry. He never showed favoritism nor cowered; he didn't appease nor flatter. He didn't try to endear others to himself nor win them over with false comfort. Because he was unconcerned with the praise of men, he was not controlled by what they thought of him. But this didn't mean he spoke carelessly. On the contrary, every word Jesus spoke flowed from a heart of love. Even his stern rebukes to the Pharisees were an incredible act of love for them, attempting to awaken them to their hypocrisy and lead them to the life that could only be found in him.

Jesus' words flowed from a heart rooted in the Father's love and his mission to restore humanity back to himself. So, on a practical level, what does it look like to reflect Christ's heart in our speech? In the following section, we will explore three overarching characteristics of transformed speech. Transformed speech is *Hospitable, Charitable* and *Restorative*. And while these aren't specific to women, they are deeply intertwined with God's calling on our lives as women. Remember, we were created to reflect the *ezer* nature of God; he created us to bring strength and aid in the context of relationship. This means how we speak and what we speak is essential to us accomplishing what God has for us and others.

HOSPITABLE

If you remember from Chapter 1, one of the attributes of God's character entrusted to us as women is the capacity to be inviting. One of the ways we reflect God's inviting nature is through verbal hospitality. *Hospitable speech is inviting, inclusive speech which helps another feel welcome and safe in your presence.*

The apostle Paul challenged the Colossian church to, "Live wisely among those who are not believers, and make the most of every opportunity" and "Let your conversation be gracious and attractive so that you will have the right response for everyone" (Colossians 4:5-6). When I reflect on those verses, a couple of things stand out to me. First, Paul's exhortation is to live wisely among those who are not believers. How often do we speak carelessly or thoughtlessly, paying no attention to who might be around us? We carelessly talk about issues like abortion or homosexuality or race, giving no thought to those who might be around us feeling isolated, wounded, and shamed by our words. We exercise our freedom of speech, often at the expense of others. We act like the babbling fool in the book of Proverbs whose words bring ruin (Proverbs 10:8,10,14). Jesus warned us that a day will come when we will have to give an account for every careless word we speak (Matthew 12:36) and yet we continue to live thoughtlessly where our words are concerned.

Some of us find it relatively easy to be more intentional and mindful of our speech when we are in spiritual places or with spiritual people. But our everyday speech often reveals more about us. Living wisely means we give serious thought to what we say, whether we are at church, at a barbeque, or talking with coworkers. We need to take time to think before we post a status or comment online. Sometimes it means we need to refrain from speech; it isn't necessary to speak everything we think or feel.

We need to remember that as Christians, we are a visible representation to the world of who Jesus is and what he stands for. It's heartbreaking to know how my careless words have cast a negative shadow on him, and how others may reject who Jesus is and what he stands for because of something I've said. Paul's challenge to live wisely—to be thoughtful, intentional, and discerning in what and how we speak—is one we would do well to heed, among believers and unbelievers alike—so we may be ready to speak into someone's life when an opportunity presents itself.

The second thing to note in Paul's exhortation to the Colossians is our speech should be *gracious* and *attractive*. A gracious host extends kindness and goes out of their way to make others feel welcome. Similarly, gracious words are pleasant; they are warm and welcoming. And just as an attractive person can be appealing and magnetic, attractive speech draws others in rather than repelling them.

Paul's command to speak in a way that is gracious and attractive means our speech must be *hospitable*. Below are a few examples of what hospitable speech looks like:

- Speaks winsomely and attractively
- Creates safety with words
- Chooses words carefully, so no one is isolated
- Uses inclusive speech, which refrains from whispering or sharing inside jokes that make others feel like an outsider
- Speaks gracious and kind words
- Speaks considerate and thoughtful words, which express genuine interest in the lives of others
- Draws others into fellowship where they feel known and cared for
- Refrains from gossip and slander or speaking ill of others
- Speaks in ways that display humility, vulnerability, and transparency about her own brokenness and helps others know they aren't alone

- Speaks in ways that honor the dignity of all people, even when discussing difficult situations
- Speaks in ways that do not add to another's burdens

Ultimately the hospitable words flowing from her mouth are sourced from her heart, which has been captivated by a gracious God who has been hospitable toward her. As a result, people want to be in her presence.

Questions for Reflection

1. Before moving on to the next section, take some time to think back over the words you've spoken in the past few weeks—especially the words you've spoken to those you are the most comfortable with.

- Was your speech hospitable? Would others characterize your words as gracious or attractive?
- Was your speech full of negativity or grumbling?
- Were yours words argumentative or divisive? Were they judgmental or critical?
- Did you use your words in crude or crass ways that might have made others uncomfortable?
- Did you make inappropriate comments or jokes at another's expense?
- What words did you use when speaking about someone from a different cultural, ethnic, or socioeconomic background? Do you flippantly make racial or ethnic jokes that demean and dehumanize?

WE CANNOT FULFILL

THE GREAT COMMISSION

WITHOUT OUR WORDS.

CHARITABLE

When you see the word charitable, what immediately comes to mind? Do you think about giving money to the poor or food to the hungry or shelter to those who need refuge? To be charitable is to give out of your own abundance to someone who is in need, whether they deserve it or not, and even when they have nothing to offer you in return. With that in mind, *charitable speech is generous with others by speaking in ways that extend the same lavish grace, mercy, patience, tolerance, and forgiveness you have so freely been given in Christ.* Paul provides a good look at what it means to be charitable with one another:

> Since God chose you to be the holy people he loves, you must clothe yourselves with tenderhearted mercy, kindness, humility, gentleness, and patience. Make allowance for each other's faults, and forgive anyone who offends you. Remember, the Lord forgave you, so you must forgive others. Above all, clothe yourselves with love, which binds us all together in perfect harmony. And let the peace that comes from Christ rule in your hearts. For as members of one body you are called to live in peace.

> Colossians 3:12–15a

Paul reminded the Colossians how charitable God had been to them and that because of God's great love, they were to "act toward others as God in Christ has acted toward them." [2] If we pause long enough to reflect, we know how remarkably charitable God has been toward us. We have not done anything to merit his favorable attitude, and yet he has lavished us with mercy, patience, kindness, and forgiveness. So we ought to be charitable toward one another.

A woman who is charitable in her speech practices Jesus' command to extend love and mercy, not only to friends and loved ones, but also to those who have harmed her:

> Love your enemies, do good to those who hate you, bless those who curse you, pray for those who abuse you . . . If you love those who love you, what benefit is that to you? For even sinners love those who love them. And if you do good to those who do good to you, what benefit is that to you? For even sinners do the same . . . But love your enemies, and do good, and lend, expecting nothing in return, and your reward will be great, and you will be sons of the Most High, for he is kind to the ungrateful and the evil. Be merciful, even as your Father is merciful.

Luke 6:27b–28,32–33,35–36 ESV

To bless rather than curse doesn't diminish or negate the offense. It is a choice, though, to entrust the offense to God and release your desires for justice on your own terms. It requires a purposeful moving toward forgiveness.

This reminds me of a valuable lesson a mentor once taught me. She taught that whenever someone hurt or offended me, I should pray for them everyday for two weeks. But I wasn't to pray just any prayer. I was to pray that God's generosity would overflow onto them, that he would bless them with everything I want and more. That was over twenty years ago, but it is a practice that has proven beneficial throughout my life.

I remember one particular situation when someone I knew became aggressive, critical, and antagonistic toward me. At first, I was disoriented by the events, I didn't understand what was going on or why. But soon my confusion and hurt turned to outright anger, and I began to harbor bitterness and ill-will in my heart. One day after a heated interaction, I drove home with hot tears of anger rolling down my cheeks, cursing the person the whole way. But the Holy Spirit intervened and reminded me of this valuable lesson. So as soon as I got home, I opened my Bible to one of the Psalms and I began to read it out loud. It reminded me that justice and vengeance belong to the Lord alone. So I began to pray. I prayed for God to bless the person who had hurt me with a strong marriage, children who love and follow the Lord, a fruitful ministry, and sweet fellowship with him. The more specific blessings I prayed for the person, the more my anger dissipated and the more my heart warmed toward them. While the hurt was still there, I no longer had any temptation toward slander, gossip, or criticism. Nothing about the situation had changed, but God had changed my heart. I didn't feel love or affection toward them, but I definitely felt peace, forgiveness, and compassion.

Below are a few examples of what charitable speech looks like:

- Is sympathetic toward others and recognizes everyone is carrying their own heavy load

- Is compassionate, places herself in another's position

- Believes the best of others rather than assuming the worst

- Overlooks minor offenses

- Is patient with others

- Doesn't hold onto grudges or seek vengeance

- Doesn't use sarcasm or passive-aggressive comments to defend herself

- Doesn't rehash the offenses of another

- Blesses rather than curses

- Prays for her enemies

- Is willing to move through the often long and difficult process of forgiveness

- Extends grace and mercy

Ultimately charitable words flow from the heart that realizes God has forgiven her for far greater offenses than those committed against her; he has extended love, mercy, compassion, favor, and forgiveness to her, and so she is compelled to extend the same charity to others.

Questions for Reflection

1. Before moving on to the next section, take some time to think back over the words you've spoken in the past few weeks—especially the words you've spoken to those you are the most comfortable with.

- Was your speech charitable? Would others characterize your words as patient and compassionate?

- Were you quick to overlook minor offenses or did you rehash and nag others over them instead?

- How did you speak to and/or about someone, who hurt you? Were your words merciful or condemning? How so?

- Did you speak a gentle word in the midst of conflict or did you use retaliatory, inflammatory, or defensive words?

- Were you judgmental or critical of someone or something for which you were not responsible? Did you invite others into the same criticism?

RESTORATIVE

Maybe you wonder why all of this even matters. What's the big deal? Sure maybe you feel like your words need to be less hurtful, but why is it important for your speech to be hospitable and charitable? When our words are hospitable and charitable, we create an environment where restorative words flourish.

Restorative speech is constructive, corrective, and instructional speech that helps others grow in faith and spiritual maturity.

Restorative speech is part of the Great Commission. One of the final commands Jesus gave his disciples was to "go and make disciples of all the nations, baptizing them in the name of the Father and the Son and the Holy Spirit" and to "teach these new disciples to obey all the commands I have given you" (Matthew 28:18–20). *We cannot fulfill the Great Commission without our words.* And if our words are riddled with caustic and combative speech, derogatory comments, racial slurs, if it is full of gossip and slander, if it is critical or judgmental, then who will want to listen to anything we have to say about who Jesus is or the hope and freedom found in him?

The apostle Paul reiterates the second part of Jesus' commission, telling the believers in Colosse to "teach and counsel each other" with all the wisdom Christ gives (Colossians 3:17). We are not only to make disciples (evangelize), we are also to instruct one another in holiness (edify). This brings everything we've discussed about our words into full light: *the aim, the end goal of all Christian speech is to help others know Christ and grow to be more like him.* This doesn't mean there is no room for fun and frivolous conversations. It simply means the mission should always be in the forefront of our minds; informing what and how we speak as believers. Understanding the importance of this will guide and direct us so that whatever conversations we engage in— whether fun and frivolous or intentional and serious—we will speak in a way that magnifies Jesus and does not hinder the gospel.

The author of Ecclesiastes said, "The words of the wise are like cattle prods—painful but helpful. Their collected sayings are like a nail-studded stick with which a shepherd drives the sheep" (Ecclesiastes 12:11). The imagery here is beautiful. A prod, or goad, is used to make livestock move by smacking or poking them with it to guide them along the right path. By comparing the words of the wise to a goad, the author is saying that wise words—while painful—urge, guide, and encourage us along the path of life. This is the heart of restorative speech.

A friend of mine once shared a story about an interaction she had with her husband. The story struck me because it's emblematic of restorative speech. Her husband had been slandered and unjustly attacked by someone close to him for almost two years. One day he was grumbling and expressing frustration with the person who had caused him so much grief and hardship. While in many ways his feelings were justified and she hurt for him, she could see the seed of bitterness and resentment in him and was concerned for his spiritual well-being. So she respectfully and lovingly encouraged him by saying, "I know this has been hard and hurtful, but Scripture tells us forgiveness is not optional." He was somewhat frustrated by her words, so he grumbled and grunted that "he already knew that," to which she replied, "I know you know, and I don't mean to sound harsh but knowing and doing are two different things. You need to forgive him." This, of course, further frustrated him, and he shut the conversation down. The next day, after having time to think about her words, he thanked her for telling him what he needed to hear. Because my friend had spoken the truth in love, her husband was more able to receive the biblical encouragement he needed. He didn't feel disrespected or chastised; instead, he felt ennobled and convicted by her words, which ultimately helped move him back toward Jesus in this area of his life. She was functioning as a peacemaker. Restorative speech is characteristic of a peacemaker, because it will always include speaking truth in love.

Restorative words include rebuke. Jesus said, "If another believer sins, rebuke that person; then if there is repentance, forgive" (Luke 17:3). Rebuke is a form of protection for us as believers; it serves as a warning to help us in our battle against temptation and sin. It is intended to serve as correction that redirects us toward obedience. The apostle Paul tells us that on this side of eternity, we battle between the desires of our flesh and the desires of the Spirit of God living in us. The temptations of this world are powerful and alluring, and we are easily self-deceived, experts at justifying our thinking and actions. This is why rebuke is imperative in the life of a Christian.

As the Proverb says, "As iron sharpens iron, so a friend sharpens a friend" (Proverbs 27:17). You and I need others to come alongside and encourage us in obedience, perseverance, and endurance. We need others to rebuke us, to tell us when we are on a reckless path. Our words should be like cattle prods, not used out of a desire to inflict pain but in order to spur one another along the path of true life. We need people in our lives who are committed to speak loving, restorative speech. Without this kind of biblical community surrounding us—teaching us, correcting us, warning us, and leading us along the path of life—our growth in spiritual maturity will be stunted at worst and slow at best. We also need to *be* people who are committed to sharpening one another by speaking in ways that are restorative. If we aren't willing or courageous enough to speak a word of warning or correction to those in our lives for fear of their response, we are leaving them vulnerable to the desires of their flesh and the temptations of this world.

The Lord considered words of rebuke so important he warned the Israelites that withholding rebuke from their neighbors was the same as hating them in their heart. And, as a result, they would bear guilt in their neighbor's sin (Leviticus 19:17). Imagine your friend told you he was embezzling money from his employer, but you never said anything about it to the employer or anyone else. When he's arrested and it's discovered you knew about his activity, you would be held accountable in a court of law. You are culpable; you share in his guilt, not because of direct action on your part but because of your inaction.

Most people think they would speak up if their friends were committing a crime, but all too often we remain painfully silent when a friend is flirting with sin. Imagine your girlfriend constantly complains about her husband and how she wishes he was like other men. She lists out all the reasons why he isn't good enough—he doesn't pursue her heart; he doesn't treat her with respect; he doesn't help with the kids or around the house; he never compliments her, etc. And then one day, she tells you she met the most amazing man who treats her like a queen. She says he loves Jesus, is actively engaged with his kids' lives, and compliments her all the time. You can see she is in an unwise situation, one that could result in the sin of adultery, but you are uncomfortable with challenging her. You might tip-toe around the subject and ask her if she thinks it's a good idea, but whenever you do she gets defensive and flustered, so you decide not to say anything else. A few months later, you find out she is having an affair with the man, and they are both leaving their spouses and children. You may not have encouraged her sinful choices, but you didn't discourage them either. Your silence in the matter is a failure to love her well and to redirect her in obedience and faithfulness as a believer. Not all circumstances are as grievous as this, but God has entrusted us to one another. He uses us to speak truth into one another and to spur one another on toward love and good works (Hebrews 10:34).

Restorative speech is also constructive. Paul urged the Thessalonians to "encourage each other and build each other up, just as you are already doing" (1 Thessalonians 5:11). So what does the Bible mean by encourage and build up? In the past, I saw it as speaking something positive, comforting, or complimentary to someone—something that would uplift them and bring a smile to their face. While that can be true, it's only a small part of what it means to encourage or build up. I think this is where we, as women, often go astray with our words—especially with one another. There is nothing wrong with wanting to bring a smile to someone's face or to speak kind and encouraging words to them. My concern, though, is that *what we view as encouragement may be nothing more than false comfort and flattery.* As a result, our words to one another are empty of the powerful, life-giving encouragement that marked Jesus' words.

It might be helpful here to see a snapshot of what flattering speech is:

- Attempts to please someone with compliments or attention
- Gives insincere compliments
- Lies (Psalm 5:9, Proverbs 26:28)
- Shows partiality/favoritism (Job 32:21)
- Seduces (Daniel 11:32)

- Brings ruin and destruction (Psalm 5:9, Proverbs 26:28)
- Manipulates for selfish gain (Daniel 11:21)
- Boasts (Psalm 12:3)
- Demonstrates a double-heart (Psalm 12:2)
- Conceited (Psalm 36:2)
- Self-serving and deceptive (Romans 16:18)
- Self-centered

The overwhelming message of Scripture is that flattery is not helpful nor loving. In fact, Proverbs goes so far as to say that to flatter a friend is to lay a trap for their feet (Proverbs 29:5). We flatter others because we need them to like us and think well of us. *So we flatter them to in order to endear them to ourselves.* Why is this so? At the root of flattery we find fear of man, a need for approval, desire for status, or a desire to control others through manipulation. Flattery isn't about helping the other person; instead it's a selfish means to a self-centered end. But God desires for us to need others less and love them more. Instead of looking for ways to manipulate others for our own gain, we need to seek God's wisdom regarding our duty toward others. [3] God desires us to encourage one another, and biblical encouragement sometimes *demands* hard words be spoken. But this kind of encouragement and edification requires incredible wisdom and kindness. Restorative speech is constructive, not destructive. *We are not to arrogantly batter each other with the truth; we are to humbly build one another up in the truth.*

Here are a few examples of what restorative speech might look like:

- Instructs others in the truth of God's word
- Speaks truth in love
- Guides another in faithful obedience to Christ

- Corrects
- Challenges
- Rebukes
- Provides godly counsel
- Is more committed to loving others than being liked by them
- Speaks constructively, rather than critically
- Doesn't tear others down with her words, but builds them up with real nourishment
- Consoles
- Exhorts
- Speaks what others need in order to help them grow stronger

Ultimately, restorative speech strengthens and fortifies someone in their faith. It promotes growth; it is constructive and instructive speech that "builds a person up to be a suitable dwelling place for God, where the Lord is at home." [4]

Questions for Reflection

1. Before moving onto the next section, use these questions to help you reflect back over the words you've spoken in the past few weeks—especially the words you've spoken to those you are the most comfortable with.

- Did you speak constructive truth? Did it strengthen or fortify another in their faith? Or did you speak words that weakened and tore them down?

- Did you use your words to instruct another in the faith? Or did you speak in such a way that might confuse or lead another astray?

- Did you correct or warn another who was flirting with sin? Or did you withdraw or withhold truth that could redirect them?

- Did you make every effort to deliver hard truth with love? Or did you lob verbal grenades at them?

- Did you speak encouraging words of comfort and consolation that enabled another to persevere? Or were you dismissive of their struggle?

Evidence of transformed speech is speaking words that are *hospitable, charitable, and restorative.* Take a few moments to look at the table below and then answer the following questions.

HOSPITABLE WORDS	CHARITABLE WORDS	RESTORATIVE WORDS
Welcoming	Merciful	Comfort/Encourage
Kind	Overlook Offenses/ Forgive	Build up
Inclusive	Bless	Guide/Instruct/Teach
Inviting	Compassionate	Correct/Redirect/ Warn
Warm	Patient	Speak truth in love
Attractive	Responsive, instead of reactive	Constructive
Gracious	Humble	Nurture/Develop

1. What areas of transformed speech do you struggle with the most (hospitable, charitable, or restorative)? Why do you think you struggle?

2. Who do you struggle with most when it comes to transformed speech (i.e. husband, children, people who have hurt you, friends)? Why do you think you struggle in those specific relationships?

LOVE, KNOW, SPEAK, DO

Sometimes we speak words of comfort, consolation, and encouragement. Other times we speak words of rebuke, correction, and warning. As believers, we are to be committed to love one another over and above ourselves, not withholding anything that could be beneficial, but doing so with gentleness and compassion.

Restorative speech, like correction or instruction, is rarely productive outside the context of relationship. If you have not taken the time to build relational capital with the person, then it is quite possible your words will be meaningless at best or inflammatory at worst. This is where a model of personal ministry found in Paul Tripp's book, *Instruments in the Redeemer's Hands*, can be very helpful. The model,

THE AIM,

THE END GOAL OF ALL

CHRISTIAN SPEECH IS TO

HELP OTHERS KNOW CHRIST

AND GROW TO BE MORE

LIKE HIM.

commonly referred to as "Love, Know, Speak, Do", provides the building blocks of a healthy relationship wherein the work of ministry has
the most opportunity to flourish and produce fruit.

LOVE

The apostle Paul taught that at the end of our lives, the love we gen-
erously gave away is one of the few things that will remain (1 Corinthians 13:13). It's easy to love those who love us back, those who are like
us, or those who are easy to love. But Jesus calls us to also love those
who have nothing to offer us, those who are different from us, those
who are difficult to love, and those who have wounded or offended
us. How we treat one another matters to God; it's a big deal. Perhaps
John said it best, "Dear friends, since God loved us that much, we surely ought to love each other. No one has ever seen God. But if we love
each other, God lives in us, and his love is brought to full expression in
us" (1 John 4:11-12). This is too important for us to gloss over. When we
love one another—in word and deed—God's love is visible to the world.
Love is the *first* step, and the most important in relational ministry to
one another. Before doing anything else, we love. Tripp says:

> Love highlights the importance of relationship in the pro-
> cess of change. Theologians call this a covenantal model of
> change. God comes and makes a covenant with us. He com-
> mits himself to be our God and he takes us as his people. In
> the context of this relationship, he accomplishes his work of
> making us like him. As we understand the way God works in
> our lives, we realize that relationship to him is not a luxury,
> but a necessity. It is the only context in which the lifelong pro-
> cess of change can take place. In the same way, we are called
> to build strong relationships with others. God's purpose is
> that these relationships would be workrooms in which his
> work of change can thrive. [5]

It's often been said that people don't care how much you know until they know how much you care. As trite as that phrase sounds, the truth of it remains. You must do the hard work of forging relationships, making investments in a person over an extended period of time, in order to have a credible voice in his or her life.

KNOW

The second step is knowing the person you are talking to. Knowing means "really getting acquainted with the people God sends our way. When you assume that you know someone, you won't ask the critical questions you need to ask to get below the surface . . . Knowing a person means knowing the heart . . . You mean that you know more about her beliefs and goals, her hopes and dreams, her values and desires. If you know your friend, you will be able to predict what she will think and how she will feel in a given situation." [6]

Knowing a person means you have studied them. You know their quirks, their pet peeves. You know their strengths and weaknesses. You know their proclivity for sin, what tempts them most. You know their personal history—what they've suffered, what baggage they are carrying, the experiences they've had that have helped shape them into who they are. You know what their relationship is like with Jesus, with his church, and with other believers.

Knowing someone means you understand who they are, what they struggle with, what makes them tick, how they've been hurt. In order to truly understand someone, you must ask questions. You must move past the superficial and into the soil of their story to see what has shaped them. When someone is talking to us, we need to be engaged enough to ask intentional questions that will help us know them better. Some examples include:

- Tell me more about that.
- How did that make you feel?

- Why do you think that upset you?
- I'm curious why you responded that way.
- What did you mean by . . . ?

This is a crucial step in personal ministry, one we cannot afford to overlook. Far too often, we jump right into giving advice, making judgments, and telling people what to do before we know anything more than superficial details about them or their situation. Knowing takes time and energy, but it is time and energy well-spent.

SPEAK

Only after we have established a loving relationship with an intimate understanding of the person do we begin to speak into their lives. If we have invested energy in the person and built relational capital in a way that demonstrates our love for and understanding of them, then we can begin to speak God's truth into them. In order to do this we ask ourselves, "'What does God want this person to see that she doesn't see? How can I help her see it?' . . . Speaking the truth in love does not mean making grand pronouncements. It means helping your friend see her life clearly. For lasting change to take place, your friend must see herself in the mirror of God's word. She also needs to see God and the resources for change that he has provided in Christ." [7]

According to Tripp, as believers, this means:

- Speaking truth is not optional
- Speaking truth after you love and know, not before
- Speaking truth to yourself first
- Speaking truth is a lifestyle not just an event
- Failing to speak truth is hatred, not love
- Speaking truth with the right goals (redemption vs. condemnation)

- Speaking the truth of the gospel: give grace and hope [8]

A GRID FOR SPEECH

While no tool of man can replace the wisdom and direction of the Holy Spirit in our lives, there is a tool—a grid for speech—we can use to guide us. Before we speak, we should ask ourselves:

- Is what I am about to say *true*?
- If it is true, is it *necessary* that I speak it?
- If it is true *and* necessary, is it *kind*?

Remember, not every true thing needs to be spoken. The gauge is whether or not it is helpful or beneficial to the person you are speaking to. It may be true, and it may be necessary, but if it is delivered in a way that is unkind, then it is ultimately not beneficial. What we say is just as important as *how* and *why* we say it. It is important to check our motives before speaking. Are the words you are about to speak rooted in love and kindness for your neighbor, or are they rooted in things like a critical spirit, jealousy, frustration, or bitterness?

This brings to mind two different occasions when the true, necessary, and kind grid could have been helpful for me. The first one was several years ago with a young woman I was mentoring. She had fallen into an unhealthy pattern of thinking, which was spilling out in words that were divisive and harmful to others as well as herself. As I listened to her speak, I became more and more angry. Some of it was righteous anger, some of it wasn't. Finally, after listening for a while, I launched into a verbal onslaught of correction and warning. That conversation didn't end well. She was wounded and defensive. I was angry and full of self-righteous indignation. Looking back on the conversation, I can see where I went astray. What I said to her that day was true. It was also necessary. Loving her well in that moment meant not abdicating the opportunity to speak corrective words. But I failed to speak with kindness. My words of warning were harsh and condemning, not humble and loving. Speaking with kindness may or may not have altered the outcome of our conversation—that would have depended on the condition of her heart at the time. But my failure to speak with kindness certainly did not create the best environment for us to have a fruitful and God-honoring conversation.

In that instance, I was the one speaking, but I've also been on the receiving end. At one point in time, I had asked a friend to give me some feedback on something I had been working on. A few weeks later she returned to give me her thoughts. The more I heard what she had to say, the more deflated and hurt I felt. I fought the temptation to get angry and be dismissive, but I could feel a seed of bitterness being planted in my heart. It took me several days to process through all she had said, weeding through my own insecurities, fears of inadequacy, and frustration with her delivery. As I was able to see more clearly, I spent some time reflecting on her feedback. Much of what she had said to me was true and necessary, and as a result would be helpful for me in the long run. But the way she said it was sharp, critical, and unkind. Because I knew her, I knew she didn't mean to be harsh, but it still took me several days of prayer and self-examination to be able to see and receive the good in what she said.

Even though I eventually saw the good in what my friend said, there is still lingering hurt. Remember words are sticky; it's hard to shake them. Taking time to evaluate our words through the grid of *true, necessary, and kind* can help create the best opportunity for our words to produce good fruit, bringing life to the other person, rather than death.

DO

Finally, Tripp says, "you must help your friend DO something with what she learns—to apply the insights God has given to her daily life and relationships. Insight alone is not change; it's only the beginning. Insights about who we are, who God is, and what he has given us in

Christ must be applied to the practical, specific realities of life. God calls your friend not just to be a hearer of his Word, but to be an active doer of it as well." [9]

Conflict in our conversations happens when the action is out of order. We begin speaking without first understanding or loving. We start giving direction and trying to move people before they know that we love them and have their highest good in view. If we hope to speak into other's lives in redemptive ways, it's important that we consider and apply these truths to our conversations.

At the end of 1 Thessalonians, Paul urges the members of the church to warn those who are lazy, encourage those who are timid, take tender care of those who are weak, and to be patient with everyone (5:14). The language here is important to note. Paul acknowledges that different people need different things at different times. Different situations merit different responses. This means we will need to seek wisdom from the Father to guide us in our conversations with one another.

But it is important to remember that not all conversations will go well, which is not always your fault. You can say the right thing, with the right intent, in the right way and at the right time, but it still may not be received well because it will run through the filters of the person on the receiving end. You are responsible for what and how you speak, but you aren't responsible for how they hear and respond. If you have communicated with love and truth, then you shouldn't fret over how the message was ultimately received. Leave that to God.

Questions for Reflection

1. Think of a conversation you've had recently that didn't go well. Which part of the principle of Love, Know, Speak, Do was missing? Which one of these is hardest for you to demonstrate, Love, Know, Speak or Do? Why?

2. Can you think of a recent conversation where using the Grid for
Speech would have been helpful?

A WORD OF ENCOURAGEMENT

I have a vision. It's idealistic and romantic. And I know it isn't
entirely possible—at least not until Jesus returns. But still I hope and
pray toward that end. I have a vision of what it would look like if all of
us lived as kingdom women. Women who have been transformed by
the love of Christ and now long to extend that same love to one another.
Women who sound like Jesus—full of grace and truth. Women who use
their words to bless and not curse; who build up and not tear down.
Women who give others the gift of being slow to speak, quick to hear,
and slow to anger. Women who overlook offenses and believe the best
of others. Women who are courageous enough to speak the truth to
one another, but do so in ways that are full of love, mercy, compassion,
kindness. Women who run alongside one another and encourage one
another to press on in faith and obedience. Women who speak in ways
that are hospitable, charitable, and restorative—whose words nurture
life and strength in those around them.

This is what God created us to do. More than that, it's who he created us to be. And while sin has broken and corrupted what God created,
it does not get the last word. Jesus has already begun a new work. He
is recreating you in his image—transforming you bit by bit, from one
degree of glory to another (2 Corinthians 3:18). By his Holy Spirit, he
has given you new life with new power, new potential and new hope so

that you can do the good work God has for you—the work of bringing strength and life to those around you.

While we will not entirely win the battle of the tongue, we can make significant progress with the Lord's help. My prayer is that we would be women committed to praying for the Lord to transform our hearts and minds so that the words we speak bring life.

Now may the God of peace—who brought up from the dead our Lord Jesus, the great Shepherd of the sheep, and ratified an eternal covenant with his blood—may he equip you with all you need for doing his will. May he produce in you, through the power of Jesus Christ, every good thing that is pleasing to him. All glory to him forever and ever! Amen. (Hebrews 13:20-21)

NOTES

CHAPTER 1

1. Grace Church and Chrystie Cole, *Biblical Femininity* (Greenville, SC: Ambassador International, 2015), 21-22.

2. See *Biblical Femininity: Discovering Clarity and Freedom in God's Design for Women* for more about the ezer calling, the core capacities of invite, nurture, and partner, autonomy, and self-protection and self-promotion

CHAPTER 2

1. Susannah Heschel, ed., Introduction to *Moral Grandeur and Spiritual Audacity, Essays Abraham Joshua Heschel* (New York: Farrar, Straus and Giroux, 1996), viii-ix.

2. "Watch your thoughts;" Pass It On, accessed January 3, 2019, https://www.passiton.com/inspirational-quotes/3869-watch-your-thoughts-for-they-become

CHAPTER 4

1. Shari Horner (friend and Grace Church member) in discussion with the author, April 10, 2015.

CHAPTER 5

1. Amy Carmichael, *If* (Fort Washington, PA: CLC Publications, 1938), 35.

2. Jim Collins, *Good to Great,* (New York: HarperCollins Publishers Inc., 2001), 69-70.

3. Collins, *Good to Great,* 72.

4. Sinclair B. Ferguson, "The Bit, the Bridle, and the Blessing: An Exposition of James 3:1-12" in *The Power of Words and the Wonder of God,* ed. John Piper and Justin Taylor (Wheaton, IL: Crossway, 2009), 48.

5. Edward Welch, *When People are Big and God is Small* (Phillipsburg, NJ: Presbyterian and Reformed Publishing Company, 1997), 23.

6. Blaise Pascal, *Pensées* (Grand Rapids, MI: Christian Classics Ethereal Library, 2002), 80, http://www.ccel.org/ccel/pascal/pensees.html

7. Paul David Tripp, "War of Words: Getting to the Heart for God's Sake" in *The Power of Words and the Wonder of God,* ed. John Piper and Justin Taylor (Wheaton, IL: Crossway, 2009), 32.

CHAPTER 6

1. Louann Brizendine, *The Female Brain* (New York: Three Rivers Press, 2006), 5.

2. Brizendine, *The Female Brain,* 8.

3. Brizendine, *The Female Brain,* 36.

4. Brizendine, *The Female Brain,* 37.

5. Ray Ortlund, "Gossip," *The Gospel Coalition* (blog), May 18, 2009, accessed April 3, 2017, https://blogs.thegospelcoalition.org/rayortlund/2009/05/18/gossip/

6. "7400. rakil," Bible Hub, accessed January 3, 2019, http://biblehub.com/hebrew/7400.htm

7. "5372. nirgan," Bible Hub, accessed January 3, 2019, http://biblehub.com/hebrew/7372.htm

8. Tremper Longman III and David E. Garland, ed., *The Expositor's Bible Commentary: Proverbs–Isaiah Vol. 6* (Grand Rapids, MI: Zondervan, 2008), 164.

9. Ortlund, "Gossip".

10. D. A. Carson et al., ed., *The New Bible Commentary Letters* (Downers Grove, IL: InterVarsity Press USA, 1994), 108.

11. "Larger Catechism: Questions 141–150," Reformed Forum, accessed January 3, 2019, https://reformedforum.org/larger-catechism-questions-141-150/

CHAPTER 7

1. Grace Church and Chrystie Cole, *Biblical Femininity* (Greenville, SC: Ambassador International, 2015), 99.

2. "4020. periergazomai," Bible Hub, accessed April 13, 2017, http://biblehub.com/greek/4020.htm

3. John R. W. Stott, *The Message of Timothy & Titus* (Downers Grove, IL: InterVarsity Press USA, 1996), 142.

CHAPTER 8

1. Bruce Demarest and Keith J. Matthews, ed., *Dictionary of Everyday Theology and Culture* (Colorado Springs, CO: NavPress, 2010), 291-293.

2. "7965. shalom," Bible Hub, accessed May 17, 2017, http://biblehub.com/hebrew/7965.htm

3. Matthews, *Dictionary of Everyday Theology and Culture*, 291-293

4. Leyland Ryken, James C, Wilhoit, and Tremper Longman III, ed., *Dictionary of Biblical Imagery* (Downers Grover, IL: Inter-Varsity Press USA, 1998), 632-33

5. "5046. Teleios," Bible Hub, accessed May 17, 2017, http://bible-hub.com/greek/5046.htm

6. Timothy Keller, *The Meaning of Marriage* (New York: Penguin Books, 2011), 48.

7. Megan Phelps-Roper, TED Talks, *I Grew up in the Westboro Baptist Church. Here's why I left,* video, 15:17, February 2017, https://www.ted.com/talks/megan_phelps_roper_i_grew_up_in_the_westboro_baptist_church_here_s_why_i_left

CHAPTER 9

1. C.S. Lewis, *The Weight of Glory* (New York, NY: Harper Collins, 2001), 26.

2. Dick Lucas, *The Message of Colossians & Philemon* (Downers Grove, IL: Intervarsity Press USA, 1980), 151.

3. Welch, *When People are Big and God is Small*, 19.

4. "3619. oikodomé," Bible Hub, accessed July 21, 2017, http://biblehub.com/greek/3619.htm

5. Paul David Tripp, *Instruments in the Redeemer's Hands* (Phillipsburg, NJ: P & R Publishing, 2002), 110.

6. Tripp, *Instruments in the Redeemer's Hands*, 111-112.

7. Tripp, *Instruments in the Redeemer's Hands*, 111-112.

8. Brian Hedges, "Instruments in the Redeemer's Hands by Paul David Tripp (Book Notes)," *Brian G. Hedges* (blog), March 14, 2010, http://www.brianghedges.com/2010/03/instruments-in-redeemers-hands-notes.html

9. Tripp, *Instruments in the Redeemer's Hands*, 112.

For more information about our other studies

BIBLICAL FEMINITY

REDEEMING SEXUALITY

BODY MATTERS

SHAME: FINDING FREEDOM

please visit:

www.GraceChurchSC.org
info@gracechurchsc.org

Made in United States
Orlando, FL
27 June 2022

19199097R00113